FAITHFUL MOMMY

Parenting With a Heart of Praise

A 60-Day Devotional for Moms

by
Kaelin Scott

ISBN: 979-8-9908775-1-1

For every mom who wants to put Jesus first

Let Him be your strength and joy

INTRODUCTION

Motherhood is such a unique experience. Truly nothing else in life compares to the position of being a mother. Some of the highest highs and lowest lows come along with being a mom. Though it's full of changes, trials, tears, and sleepless nights, we wouldn't trade it for anything. It's one of life's greatest blessings.

As moms, we have a responsibility to keep Christ at the heart of everything our family does. It's our sacred duty to point our families to Jesus and ensure our homes are filled with the Spirit.

But how can we approach parenting with a heart of praise when our lives are so hectic? How can we put Jesus first when we're just trying to get through the day?

There's no one right answer or perfect formula for that, but I've divided this devotional into 12 specific areas we can focus on. My desire is for this to be an edifying experience that fills you with hope and joy.

As a mom, you are in the beautiful position of pointing your family to Christ, and my guess is that you take that responsibility seriously. Otherwise, you probably wouldn't have picked up this book! My prayer is that these 60 days will be an encouragement to you as you walk through motherhood hand in hand with Jesus.

So, if you're with me, let's dive in and approach parenting with a heart of praise.

Serving With Gladness

DAY 1

Do all things without complaining and disputing.
Philippians 2:14 NKJV

There's always so much to do, isn't there? Making meals, cleaning the house, driving kids around to different activities, paying bills, endless dirty dishes, piles of laundry, etc. Then add on work or other responsibilities, and life can feel pretty stressful.

It's easy to approach the daily routine with a sigh or a groan. I get it. Really, I do. I've been there so many times.

Sometimes it feels like there's too much to do and not enough time. Every time I check one thing off my to-do list, another five things get added on, making me feel like I'll never finish it all. All I want to do is sit down and rest, but I never have time to relax. And even if I do, I feel guilty because there are other things I could be doing instead.

A lot of times, mom life feels like a chore. But treating it that way is not honoring to God. We're not being good stewards of all our many blessings if we're constantly grumbling or complaining. Imagine giving your children a beautiful gift, but all they did was fuss and complain about it instead of being thankful. That's essentially how we treat God when we face our responsibilities with a negative attitude.

Instead of looking at all we have to do as a burden, as Christians, we can choose to filter it through the lens of joy. Those dirty dishes are in the sink because I was blessed enough to share a meal with my family. That laundry basket is overflowing because my active children had a lot of fun getting their clothes dirty. I'm tired because I'm living a life full of love. What a joy these things are to me!

Sometimes love feels like chaos. But isn't it a beautiful kind of chaos? Isn't a house full of laughter and messiness much better than a tidy house filled with silence? Aren't those giggles and snuggles and kisses worth all the work that goes into being a mom? I'm guessing you're smiling and nodding your head with a resounding *yes*.

This life is a gift. Make it your mission to see the blessings. I'm betting you won't be able to keep count, and you'll find yourself smiling more too.

Lord, thank you for my precious family. Help me to see them through your eyes. Help me to recognize my many blessings and to be a good steward of all you have given me. Forgive me for my grumbling and complaining. Fill me with joy as I face the tasks ahead. You are so good to me.
In Jesus's Name, Amen

DAY 2

Serve wholeheartedly, as if you were serving the Lord, not people.
Ephesians 6:7 NIV

Service is a word that gets a bad rap. These days, telling a woman to serve her family is akin to forcing her to be taken advantage of. But when we have a Christlike attitude, we don't view service as something forced upon us. Instead, it becomes an act of love and a form of ministry. Jesus Himself came to serve others, and He expects the same from us, starting with our own families.

Serving our families doesn't mean we are their slaves or their maids. It doesn't turn us into a doormat that gets trampled on and beaten down. It means that we pour our hearts into making sure the ones we love are taken care of well. It's giving them our all because they mean everything to us, just as Jesus did for us. He modeled a heart of humble servitude as He walked the earth, and that's exactly how we should approach our role as mothers.

Something I've found to be true is exactly what today's verse tells us. If we work as if we're doing it for Jesus, it makes it easier and more fulfilling. When we do everything in service to Jesus, we do it wholeheartedly because we're doing it for the living God who loves us beyond compare. He gave His all for us, and He deserves our best in return.

When we're tired, when we're hopeless, when we feel like collapsing under the weight of it all – that's when we can choose to go one step further. We can keep on giving. Not out of our own strength, but out of the abundance of joy and faithfulness He so graciously extends to us. We can imagine Jesus standing right next to us while we work, smiling because we love our families so well.

Yes, we're serving our families. But in so doing, we are ultimately serving the Lord. And there is nothing more beautiful or important than that.

Father, thank you for the privilege of serving my family, knowing that I am serving you too. Help me to work as if I am working for you alone, giving my all to you just as you gave your all to me. Thank you for the tasks you've given me for today. To you be all the glory, now and forever.
In Jesus's Name, Amen

DAY 3

Serve the Lord with gladness; come before His presence with singing.
Psalm 100:2 NKJV

Today's verse gives us two practical ways to make service into worship. First, we must serve with gladness. Simple, right? Just be glad!

Okay, I know. Easier said than done. But something I tell my kids often – and I'm sure you do too – is that we can choose to change our bad attitude. As hard as it is to admit sometimes, this applies to us grown-ups too. Sometimes we feel grouchy about the tasks set before us, but we can absolutely change that sour mood into an attitude of joy. We *get* to do all these things because God has blessed us with a family to care for, and that should make us glad.

The second part of the verse says to come before His presence with singing, and I think that actually helps with the first part. Whenever I *really* don't want to do the dishes (which is honestly most of the time), I crank up some worship music and jam along. It helps me get in a better mood, and before long I start paying more attention to singing than to scrubbing the dishes. It's hard to be grouchy when you're worshiping because praising Jesus cancels out the monotony of the job.

Making service into worship is as simple as changing your heart toward the job you have to do. It has to get done anyway, but your attitude toward doing it is completely up to you. A poor attitude only makes the job less enjoyable, but an attitude of gladness makes it into an act of worship.

Choosing worship sets the tone for your day, and often for your family too. You'll find that joy is contagious, bringing a more peaceful atmosphere to your home. Isn't that a beautiful thing?

Lord Jesus, thank you for the chance to serve you today. Help me to do it with gladness and rejoicing. Let my service become an act of worship as I focus my heart on you. You alone are worthy of my praise, and you've given me so much to be thankful for.
In Jesus's Name, Amen

DAY 4

Let nothing be done through selfish ambition or conceit, but in lowliness of mind let each esteem others better than himself. Let each of you look out not only for his own interests, but also for the interests of others.

Philippians 2:3-4 NKJV

If you spend any amount of time on social media, chances are you'll see posts exalting the concept of "self-care." The typical buzzwords are along the lines of "me time" and "treat yourself." Basically, people have begun promoting the idea of putting yourself first.

There's not a lot of alone time when you're a mom. It doesn't matter if your kids are toddlers or teenagers – they always find some way to invade your space, and they keep you busy pretty much every waking hour. So it's understandable to need a little bit of down time every once in a while. There's nothing wrong with taking care of yourself or giving yourself time to rest.

However, our culture is not truly advocating self-care in its true definition, but rather using the phrase as justification for putting oneself first. It's glorified selfishness, and it's the complete opposite of what we are called to do.

Our calling, as mothers and as Christians in general, is to put others before ourselves. It's countercultural, it's against our flesh nature, and sometimes it's just not very fun. But it *is* pleasing to our Heavenly Father. Not only does it glorify Him, but it also gives Him the chance to be our sustenance. It allows us to rely more fully on Him, which fosters a deeper ability to find our satisfaction solely through Him.

When we empty ourselves to serve others, we find a peaceful satisfaction in knowing we've served our Father well. And just when we think we have nothing left to give, He fills us with His powerful presence and strength, allowing us to go farther than we ever thought possible.

What we need isn't more "me-time." It's more time being filled with Jesus, so we have more love to pour into others.

Lord Jesus, please help me to crucify the fleshly desire to serve myself. Give me your strength and your heart for others. Help me to serve my family well and put their needs before my own, just as you did for me. Thank you for filling me in a way that nothing else ever could. You are all I need.
In Jesus's Name, Amen

DAY 5

Let all that you do be done with love.
1 Corinthians 16:14 NKJV

There are times when taking care of my family feels more like a chore than something I enjoy doing. So much work goes into being a mom that it can start to become an obligation rather than a joyful passion. I find myself hurrying through each task just so I can check another box off my list, ready to get to the end of the day so I can finally get some rest.

But if I slow down and focus on seeing my life through a heavenly lens, I realize that these tasks aren't burdens. They're acts of love in the form of service.

One thing I get really exhausted by is constantly having to figure out what to cook for dinner. Then there's the actual cooking part. And don't forget the worst part of all – cleaning up after all is said and done. It's easy to look at that as a burden or just another duty I have to perform. But it becomes so much easier, so much more joy-filled, when I approach it from a place of love.

I love my family, so I want to make them delicious and healthy food. I love my family, so I want to prepare a nice meal to eat together at the end of the day. Because I love my family, I don't mind cleaning up after cooking them a meal. I am blessed because I *get* to do all these things for the people I love.

As we serve our families, our greatest motivator should not be obligation. It should always, always be love. Everything we do should be done out of the love that overflows from our hearts. Our families are our greatest blessings, and love should be the force that drives us to serve them well.

As you go about your day today, tackle each task with joy as you focus on how much God loves you, and how much you love your family.

Heavenly Father, thank you for loving me so selflessly. Thank you for your service because of that love. Help me to love my family well, and let that love shine forth in all that I do. Lord, let me never tire of loving the ones you've entrusted to me.
In Jesus's Name, Amen

Posture of Prayer

DAY 6

Rejoice always, pray continually, give thanks in all circumstances; for this is God's will for you in Christ Jesus.
1 Thessalonians 5:16-18 NIV

If I'm being totally honest, it's usually easy for me to find something to complain about, or at least something I wish was better. Things in my house are falling apart, there's clutter in every room, and all the things I have to do keep piling up without end. Sometimes I'm just sick of it all.

Normally when I feel like this, though, I get a heavy dose of conviction. After looking around at all that I deem *wrong* with my life, it dawns on me that I should be focusing on everything *right*. Because the truth is that I have a lot to be thankful for.

At the top of that list is my sweet family, the absolute most precious gift in the whole entire world. I should be praising God and thanking Him for such a wonderful blessing, not looking at all the things I wish I could change. Life is so much brighter when I choose rejoicing over complaining. Things will never be perfect, so what better time to be thankful than right now, in this moment?

Gratitude should be on the tip of our tongues every day as we cover our loved ones in prayer, knowing that God has entrusted them to us to care for. How can we not be thankful when we realize what a gift that is? We should be continually rejoicing and thanking Him for our precious children.

His will for us is to be filled with a spirit of love and joy toward our families. Yes, the hard and tiring days will come. There will be many days where we feel overwhelmed and exhausted. But that doesn't erase the necessity of giving thanks.

Rejoicing is great medicine for a bad attitude. Sometimes a shift in perspective is all we need in order to see that there is so much to be grateful for.

Lord Jesus, thank you so much for my beautiful family. Thank you for entrusting them to me. Please revive my spirit of joy and help me to rejoice today, no matter what I might face. You are so gracious to me, Father. Thank you for the blessings all around me. In Jesus' Name, Amen

DAY 7

Do not be anxious about anything, but in every situation, by prayer and petition, with thanksgiving, present your requests to God.
Philippians 4:6 NIV

Think about the word *anxious*. What feelings does it evoke? Probably not many good ones.

It seems like being a mom makes anxiety a hundred times more prevalent in our everyday lives. There's so much to worry about and fret over. We want our families to be well taken care of, and it can feel like a lot of pressure weighing down on us to keep everything running smoothly.

But walking with Jesus means that we don't have to carry the weight on our own. We don't have to be anxious or afraid. We can lay it all at His feet, knowing that He can carry it for us. There is comfort in knowing that He is in control.

No matter what challenges might arise in our homes, we can bring our every worry to Jesus. As much as we love our children, He loves them even more. They are *His* children even more than they are ours, and He takes good care of His children. We can trust Him to be both our Father as well as theirs.

God already knows everything we're stressed about, so why not bring it before Him in prayer? Whether things are going well or everything's falling apart, He wants us to draw near to Him. We can always approach His throne and know that He will hear us, and we can confidently seek His help in every situation.

When obstacles present themselves today, make a conscious effort to bring your concerns to God. Place them in His hands and trust Him to work it all out.

Instead of embracing anxiety, rest in the embrace of the God who loves you – and your family – beyond measure.

Father God, please banish all anxiety from my heart today. Fill me with your peace that surpasses all understanding. I lay my worries at your feet because I know you are in control and I trust you. Please watch over my family and comfort me as I care for them.
In Jesus' Name, Amen

DAY 8

And pray in the Spirit on all occasions with all kinds of prayers and requests.
Ephesians 6:18a NIV

Thinking about the future can be daunting, especially when you think about all the unknowns your children might face. What challenges will they walk through? What tough choices will they have to make? It can be overwhelming trying to imagine who they will become and what they will make of their lives.

As their mothers, we must stay in tune with the Holy Spirit. We must seek the Spirit's guidance as we pray over our children each day.

Sometimes we know what's going on and exactly what to pray about. Other times it might be more confusing, or we might be in the dark about certain situations. That's when we can appeal to God through the power of the Holy Spirit and pray Spirit-led prayers. We can bring our children before the throne of God and cover them in prayer, trusting that He is working mightily in their lives.

Nothing is hidden from His sight. He knows exactly what our children need, even when we don't. The future is not some grand mystery to God. He knows who our kids will become and the purpose He has for their lives, and He will be with them every step they take, every single day. The God of the universe is walking alongside them, even as they step into the unknown and spread their wings outside of our homes.

As a mom, it's so comforting to know that our children will never have to walk through life alone, and through that knowledge we should be emboldened as we pray for them.

Heavenly Father, thank you for your presence in my life as well as the lives of my children. Thank you that their futures are secure in you, and that you are with them wherever they go. Keep me in tune with the Spirit as I seek your guidance and pray for my children today.

In Jesus' Name, Amen

DAY 9

The Lord is far from the wicked, but He hears the prayer of the righteous.
Proverbs 15:29 NKJV

I once heard a pastor say that he wasn't sure if God heard his prayers, and my stomach dropped to my knees. I couldn't believe something so faithless could be said from the pulpit. How dismal for a leader of the church to question whether his prayers were truly heard!

Thankfully, dear moms, we don't have to wonder whether He hears us or not. The answer is a resounding *yes.* Every word we utter, every heartfelt cry we lift, every tearful, desperate plea – He hears them all. Not only that, but He cares deeply about every single one. Our prayers are music to His ears, a pleasing aroma that arises from our hearts.

All who belong to Jesus are children of the Most High, and He hears His children when they cry out to Him. So we can boldly and confidently approach Him with anything that troubles our hearts. We can offer up our hearts to Him, no matter how broken or bruised.

Being a mother, I find this even more comforting because sometimes, there are problems I simply can't solve. I'm only a human being. I can't fix everything for my kids. I can't make everything better.

But I know the God who can do anything, and I know that He is listening. He is active and involved in my life, and the same is true for my children. He is the only One who can fix their broken pieces, the only One who can take away their shame, and the Only one who can put them back together when their hearts are shattered.

The prayer of a righteous mother is a powerful tool. Our children need us to fight for them on our knees.

God Almighty, thank you for always hearing my prayers. I know that my cries never fall on deaf ears. I trust you to answer my prayers in your timing. Your ways are higher than my ways, Lord. Please watch over and care for my family. I give you control and trust your plan, whatever it may be.
In Jesus' Name, Amen

DAY 10

"So I say to you, ask, and it will be given to you; seek, and you will find; knock, and it will be opened to you."
Luke 11:9 NKJV

Have you ever prayed for something and felt like God didn't answer? Maybe you waited a little while, but then nothing happened, so you gave up on praying about it.

I've been there. There are relationships in my life I've prayed over for years. I've begged God for healing and reconciliation, but it still hasn't happened. I've poured out my heart countless times, but things are still the same.

Sometimes it's tempting to think He's not answering our prayers. Our finite human minds don't understand His reasoning, so we assume He doesn't care. But the truth is that He always answers us – sometimes we just don't like what He has to say.

Yet it's not our place to tell God what should happen. Our job is simply to keep calling on Him – to keep bringing our hearts to Him – and trust that His plan is best.

Regardless of the outcome, we must never stop asking. We must never stop seeking. We must never stop knocking. We must never stop praying for our families.

God knows which doors to open. He knows much better than we do. Still, just because He already knows, that doesn't mean He doesn't want us to bring our requests to Him. He desires our prayers, and He is waiting for us to come and knock on the door.

He has all the answers laid out before Him. He sees our hearts and knows our minds. Though we may never get the full picture until we reach heaven, we can trust Him to answer our prayers in the best way.

Never stop asking, never stop seeking, and never stop knocking. Trust that He knows what He's doing. Your life is in His hands.

Precious Jesus, thank you for being attentive to my cries. Lord, open the doors you want me to walk through, and keep the other doors shut. Open my heart to your guidance as I cover my family in prayer. I know that your plan is best, and I trust you.
In Jesus' Name, Amen

Love Like Jesus

DAY 11

And above all, love each other deeply, because love covers over a multitude of sins.
1 Peter 4:8 NIV

If you watch chick flicks or rom-coms, you've likely seen lots of cheesy movies. The storylines vary, but the gist is usually the same – guy and girl fall in love, overcome some obstacle standing in their way, and live happily ever after. The romantic way these stories portray love is exciting, and yes, romance like that can be real.

But there's so much more to love than that.

Love often starts out as a feeling, but it can't last on feelings alone. Real and deep love is choosing someone over and over again, sacrificing your own needs for theirs, and wanting the absolute best for them. It's a daily decision to be loyal to someone and stand by them no matter what.

It can be hard to love our families sometimes. They get on our last nerve and push every button we have. We start feeling like we give more than we take and we just need a break. We get stuck in our feelings and want to pull our hair out because we're so overstimulated.

Don't worry, I get it. Love isn't always easy. When you spend a lot of time with someone, you're bound to get tired of each other every once in a while. It's an inevitable fact of life. Our feelings fluctuate. They ebb and flow. They're not constant or steady at all.

But that's why we don't base love on our feelings. We actively choose to love our families because Christ so graciously loves us, even though we don't deserve it one bit.

We love our families deeply. Wholeheartedly. Unconditionally. Without limits. We choose them over and over again, even when it's hard. Even when we just want to be alone for five minutes. Even when we feel like everything is falling apart.

The love we have for our families is what enables us to look past their flaws and see them through God's eyes. They are His beautiful children, His beloved creations, His precious treasure.

By His grace and through His strength, we are able to model that same heart toward our loved ones. A heart of unending forgiveness and love. A heart that reflects the love of our Savior every single day, despite our fluctuating feelings.

Holy Father, thank you for my precious family and the love they bring to my life. Enable me to see them through your eyes and love them with a heart like yours. Help me not to stand on my feelings, but on the truth of your steadfast and unfailing love for me. Lord, you are so good. Your love endures forever. In Jesus' Name, Amen

DAY 12

"Greater love has no one than this, than to lay down one's life for his friends."
John 15:13 NKJV

As a mom, you'd do pretty much anything for your kids. If it came down to it, you would even give your life for them. You're willing to go the distance to protect them and care for them because they're your children. That's a special kind of bond that nothing can break.

It's also a beautiful reminder of Christ's sacrificial love for us. We're able to love our families deeply because Christ modeled it for us. He gave His all for us, holding nothing back as He laid down His life, because we are His children. Nothing could ever keep Him from loving us – not even death itself.

How amazing is the Father's love for us. He is such a good Father, isn't He? His love is perfect. It never fails.

As earthly parents, we don't get everything right. We mess up, we fall short, and we fail. But through our mishaps and mistakes, we can still work toward exhibiting that sacrificial love. We can embrace His strength when we are weak, knowing that He will carry us through each day. His love is what will sustain us and enable us to continue loving our families.

Our children depend on us, which is why we have to depend on God. Because without His love, everything we do is meaningless. There is no greater love in all of creation than the love He has for each of us, and it is that very same love that should flow through our veins as we embrace our role as mothers.

Jesus gave it all for us, so we can give it all for our kids. There's nothing greater than that. Praise the Lord for this beautiful picture of love!

Dear Jesus, thank you for your perfect picture of love. I praise you for the sacrifice you made for me. Nothing in all of creation compares to you. Lord, I pray that your love flows through me as I serve my family today. You gave it all, so I can do the same. Hallelujah.

In Jesus' Name, Amen

DAY 13

Love is patient, love is kind. It does not envy, it does not boast, it is not proud. It does not dishonor others, it is not self-seeking, it is not easily angered, it keeps no record of wrongs. Love does not delight in evil but rejoices with the truth. It always protects, always trusts, always hopes, always perseveres.
1 Corinthians 13:4-7 NIV

These verses pretty much sum up everything love should be. In reading these words, we have a blueprint of how we should act when we truly love someone.

As we've previously discussed, love is not based on feelings. If it was, I don't think Paul would say it is not easily angered. Love is not something we *feel*, but rather something we *do*.

Love is action. It's how we treat people. It's infused into our character. If we are truly acting in love, it will be evident by the fruit we bear.

These verses are full of wonderful truths we can use to evaluate whether we're truly exhibiting love. Sometimes we need to ask ourselves the tough questions. Am I envious? Am I prideful? Am I easily angered? Do I persevere?

Regardless of your answers to those questions, a heart check is never a bad thing. Aligning yourself with Scripture is the best way to ensure that your love reflects that of Jesus.

The world will try to define love in many ways, but our definition comes from the Bible – the clearest picture of love we could ever have. If our love is based on feelings, then it's not Biblical love.

And thank God for that, because true love lasts so much longer than any feeling ever could.

Loving Father, I praise you for your eternal love. Your Word is the blueprint by which I live my life. Lord, help me to embody the love you have modeled and graciously bestowed upon me. Forgive me for my failures, and help me to look more like you.
In Jesus' Name, Amen

DAY 14

We love because He first loved us.
1 John 4:19 NIV

The only reason we're able to love at all is because God first loved us. We could not possibly know love unless God had demonstrated it for us. He alone is the perfect illustration of love.

If His love flows through our veins, then that same love should overflow to those around us. The deep and all-consuming love of the Father should be the same love we show our families. In order for God's love to be poured out of our hearts, we must first allow ourselves to be filled.

So how do we fill ourselves with His love? We spend time in His Word every day, and we intentionally carve out time for prayer. There's no specific formula or required amount of time you have to spend doing these things. It's simply giving God the firstfruits of your time and energy. It's easier to be filled with His love when it's the first thing on your mind every morning.

Before we scroll on our phones, before we turn on the news, before we get thrown into the chaos of our day, we need to come before the King and seek His voice above the noise. Our hearts aren't going to be filled with His love if we don't devote any of our time to Him. Spending quality time together is vital for a healthy relationship. Drawing close to Jesus allows His love in your heart to grow.

And that, mama, is what enables you to love your family well. Even when you're tired and stressed and at the end of your rope. Love knows no limits. We know that because God's love has no limits when it comes to us.

Today I want to remind you that God loves you so much. Nothing in this world could ever compare to the vastness of His love for *you*. You are His daughter, His precious creation, and His most beloved treasure. No matter what your day looks like today, remember that you are loved by the King of Everything.

Precious Jesus, fill my heart with your love today. Help me to draw near to you, knowing that you also will draw near to me. I pray that your love for me will overflow in the way I love my family. Thank you for the precious gift of your love.
In Jesus' Name, Amen

DAY 15

And over all these virtues put on love, which binds them all together in perfect unity.
Colossians 3:14 NIV

Love is the glue that holds everything else together. Everything we do should come from a place of love. Otherwise, it's all meaningless.

We can put on many different hats and fill many different roles, and some days it's hard to love. Our energy is zapped and our hearts are heavy. It's human nature to adopt an attitude of apathy when life is busy or hard. It's easier to be detached and aloof than to intentionally put on love.

But love should be woven into the very fabric of our existence, more than any other attribute we possess. We should be a safe place for our children to land – a peaceful presence they can always turn to in this crazy world. We should be an advocate for unity within our homes, bringing our families closer together by radiating selfless love.

It doesn't matter if I'm the smartest or the prettiest, or if I make the most money or have the nicest house, or if I'm successful or accomplished. If I'm not an active picture of love, then my labor is all in vain. If my home is not a peaceful environment, then my focus is on the wrong things.

The number one priority for my family must always be love and unity. We are a team, and we stick by each other. We have each other's backs, and we care about each other's hearts. We share in each other's joys and carry each other's burdens. We are unified under one common love that ties us all together. Our home is a place of love, centered around our Lord and Savior.

Heavenly Father, help me to put on love and promote unity in my family. May our home be filled with peace and rest, away from the noise of the world. Let your love reign in our hearts and shine a light in the darkness. Thank you for the love and unity you give us through the Father, Son, and Holy Spirit.
In Jesus' Name, Amen

Armed With the Spirit

DAY 16

But the fruit of the Spirit is love, joy, peace, forbearance, kindness, goodness, faithfulness, gentleness and self-control. Against such things there is no law.
Galatians 5:22-23 NIV

When you were a kid, did your parents ever say, "Do as I say, not as I do?" Usually people say it in a joking way or to play it off when they do something they shouldn't, but it's not actually a great motto to have.

Especially as parents, we should exhibit consistency in our behavior, not hypocrisy. We shouldn't expect our children to behave one way while completely ignoring our own standards. We can't just talk the talk – we also have to walk the walk.

Our kids should be able to expect the best from us because we bear good fruit on a daily basis, and the only way we can consistently bear good fruit is if we are walking in step with the Spirit. We cannot allow our flesh to be in control. We have to surrender ourselves to the Holy Spirit every single day.

If we are truly walking in the Spirit, it will be evident by the way we act and speak. The Spirit is full of love and joy and peace. It's patient and kind and good. Faithful and gentle and self-controlled. These are the attributes we should aim to demonstrate by the way we live our lives and the way we treat our families.

We want our children to become people who exude the Spirit. We want Christ's radiance to pour out of them as they go out into the world. Our goal as mothers is to raise Christlike boys and girls who will point others to the truth. In order to accomplish that goal, we must first be Christlike ourselves.

Our children need good examples. They need mothers who crucify their flesh, pick up their cross, and put on the Spirit every day. They need to see what it means to truly follow Jesus, and they need us to model it for them, because we are the ones with the most impact in their lives.

It's not an easy task, but it is a holy assignment. Showing our children the way is one of life's greatest purposes, and it is only through divine strength that we can succeed in this mission.

If we want to bear good fruit, then we must clothe ourselves with the Spirit.

Dear Lord, help me to bear good fruit. I pray that my life is walking proof of your goodness. Lord, help my children to choose the right paths, and help me to set a good example for them today and every day. Let my life exude your presence. Thank you for sending the Holy Spirit to help me and guide me.
In Jesus' Name, Amen

DAY 17

Put on the full armor of God, so that you can take your stand against the devil's schemes.
Ephesians 6:11 NIV

Part of our job as mothers is to protect our children from harm. We protect them from physical harm and emotional harm as best as we can, but it is equally important, if not more, to protect them from spiritual harm.

The devil is after our children. I hate to say that, but it's true. He doesn't want them to follow Jesus. He wants them to follow anything else, as long as it's not our precious Savior. He prowls around like a lion, looking to devour his prey (1 Peter 5:8). He will try to persuade our children to believe all sorts of lies, and that is why we must be armed for battle.

We must buckle up the belt of truth so that we are ready to combat the enemy's lies. We must put on the breastplate of righteousness so that we are not vulnerable to his attacks. Our feet must be fitted with readiness in order to stand firm in God's Word. We must take up the shield of faith so we can deflect the flaming arrows Satan launches at our families. We need to wear the helmet of salvation so that our minds are not easily swayed by doubt or fear. And we must take up the sword of the Spirit so that we can defeat lies with the truth.

We cannot afford to be passive as we disciple our children. We must be armed and ready to take on anything that comes our way, which means that we must be deeply and firmly rooted in our faith in what the Bible says.

Sometimes the devil's attacks are obvious because he comes in with guns a-blazing. Other times it's more subtle. He slips in through tiny cracks and worms his way into our homes.

But we already know that victory is the Lord's. We know who we belong to, and we know that He will never leave us defenseless. If we fight through the power of the Spirit, we can know with confidence that Christ's victory is our victory, and we can trust that our children are protected.

In what ways is the enemy attacking your family? Give the battle to Jesus right now. Put on your spiritual armor and fight for your family, knowing that Jesus is fighting right beside you on your behalf and victory is already His.

Heavenly Father, protect my children from the enemy's schemes. Help me to deflect the flaming arrows he throws at my family. Help me to put on the full armor of God so that I am ready for the battle. I know that victory belongs to you, and I belong to you too. You promised to never leave me, and I trust you to protect me because you always keep your promises.
In Jesus's Name, Amen

DAY 18

For God has not given us a spirit of fear, but of power and of love and of a sound mind.
2 Timothy 1:7 NKJV

God has not given us a spirit of fear. What a clear and comforting message.

I don't know about you, but fear is something I struggle with, especially fear of the unknown. The what-ifs often terrify me until I spiral out of control. I dwell on what *might* or *could* happen, even though the things I obsess over usually don't ever happen.

Why is this? Well, I don't know the answer to why I struggle with this, but I do know that it isn't from God. His word is clear – He does not give us a spirit of fear. Worry and fear are never from God. End of story.

What He *has* given me, though, is power and love and a sound mind. Whenever I'm grappling with the temptation to give in to fear, I can call out to Him instead. I can tap into the power He has given me to stand against fear. I can hold onto His perfect love that casts out fear. I can embrace the spirit of a sound mind – a mind that is steadfast and trusting in Him.

We don't always know what will happen, either in our lives or the lives of our children. It's easy to be afraid. The world is a scary place! But we don't have to know what will happen in order to be at peace. We can rest assured because we know that nothing in this world can pluck us, or our children, from our Savior's loving hand.

Whenever life throws you a curveball, don't give in to fear. Remember that you have been given a sound mind in Christ Jesus, and embrace the power of the Holy Spirit to combat the enemy's lies.

You know who holds the future, so fear has no place in your heart.

Dear Jesus, thank you for the spirit of power and love you have given me. Thank you for the blessing of a sound mind. Help me not to give in to fear, but to embrace your peaceful presence. I know that you are in control, and I trust you to care for my family.
In Jesus' Name, Amen

DAY 19

But He said to me, "My grace is sufficient for you, for my power is made perfect in weakness." Therefore I will boast all the more gladly about my weaknesses, so that Christ's power may rest on me.
2 Corinthians 12:9 NIV

Do you ever feel weak? Like you can't possibly continue on, because everything is out of control and you're exhausted and just can't carry it all anymore?

If you answered yes, I have good news for you. You don't have to be strong enough. Your weakness is exactly what enables God to work in your life. His power is displayed through the lives of His children when we realize that we simply are not strong enough.

There is such beautiful freedom in admitting that you can't handle it all on your own. Once you lay it all at His feet, giving Him control and trusting Him to move, life becomes so much richer. When you bow at His feet in surrender, He endows you with heavenly strength.

It's hard to explain it to someone who's never experienced it, but I'm sure you know what I'm talking about. Those moments when you're weak and weary, but you pray for strength, and somehow God gives you exactly what you need. It's absolutely amazing how powerful that act of surrender is.

And isn't it so beautiful knowing that we don't have to serve our families with our own strength? If that was the case, I don't know if I would survive. It takes a lot to be a wife and a mom, and I rely on the Holy Spirit to get me through every day. It is by His strength alone that I am able to accomplish the tasks laid out before me while loving my family well.

My weaknesses are opportunities to glorify Jesus, because they allow Him to work through me. And that is exactly what the world needs to see.

Lord Jesus, thank you for your strength. I know that when I am weak, then your strength works through me. Help me to walk in the freedom of surrendering my life to you. I don't have to be strong, because you are strong enough for me. Thank you for all the ways you are working in my life.
In Jesus' Name, Amen

DAY 20

Be completely humble and gentle; be patient, bearing with one another in love. Make every effort to keep the unity of the Spirit through the bond of peace.
Ephesians 4:2-3 NIV

I want my home to be described as a peaceful atmosphere. I want my family members to feel rested and secure whenever they are at home. But a peaceful household doesn't just magically happen on its own.

It requires an active effort on my part to humbly and gently serve my family. I have to be patient and kind with them, showing them love in the moments where I don't feel like it. Like when my kids are constantly at each other's throats, the house is a wreck, and I have a million things to do. That would be an easy time to lash out or be grouchy. And trust me, there are many times when that's exactly what I do.

But those are the moments when I need to call on the Holy Spirit for strength. Because if I'm trying to do it on my own, I'll fail. Utterly and completely. It's only by walking in the Spirit that I can successfully ensure an environment of peace.

As today's verse says, it's important to keep the unity of the Spirit. There is only one way for my family to be united in peace, and that's by the power of the Holy Spirit.

And that's good news! Because the Holy Spirit is not distant or disconnected from me, no matter how stressed or overwhelmed I might feel. In any circumstance or situation, I have access to the power granted to me by God through His Spirit, and so do you.

What a beautiful and comforting reminder. We don't have to strive to maintain peace on our own – we can't anyway, and we'll only wear ourselves out trying. We maintain the bond of peace by staying united under the Spirit of God.

He gives us the strength we need. He strengthens us to follow His commandments. He equips us to walk out the calling of motherhood He's placed on our lives. We have power in His Name, now and forevermore.

God Almighty, equip me with your strength as I serve my family today. Help our home to be united in the bond of peace, by the power of the Holy Spirit. Thank you for giving me access to your power to fulfill the tasks before me. In you, I can do all things.
In Jesus' Name, Amen

Trust in His Timing

DAY 21

Trust in the Lord with all your heart, and lean not on your own understanding; in all your ways acknowledge Him, and He shall direct your paths.
Proverbs 3:5-6 NKJV

Today's message is simple yet fundamental to a life of faith: Trust in Jesus.

We like to depend on ourselves to get things done. I don't think that's unique to our time period, but rather a symptom of being human. Still, it's even more prevalent in today's world, where our list of responsibilities seems to be ever-growing. Our plates are full and our burdens are heavy, and it takes a lot of careful planning and execution to make sure our ducks are all in a row.

But what if it doesn't take much at all? What if our most important task each day is simply to trust the Lord?

The world tries to tell us we need all these apps and calendars and planners to keep our lives functioning at the highest level. We want to streamline our lives to make them as efficient as we possibly can, and there are so many resources we can turn to in order to make that easier.

But we often neglect the most important resource of all – our Lord and Savior, Jesus Christ. All we need to do is trust in Him, and He will direct our paths. It's so simple, yet it goes against our very nature. We want to trust ourselves, but our understanding isn't divine. Our ways are not His ways (Isaiah 55:8).

If we want to ensure the best possible life for our families, we have to entrust them to Jesus. His plan doesn't always fit into what we envision our lives to be, but that's not the purpose of trusting Him. The reason we lean on Him is so we can look more like Him.

Our purpose in this world is not to live happy and carefree lives, though, of course, we all want to have that. Our ultimate purpose is to glorify our Maker, and we can't do that if we're too focused on making sure everything goes right.

Sometimes we just need to let go and trust that His outcome is worth waiting on.

Lord Jesus, help me to lean on you instead of my own understanding. Sometimes I don't understand your plan, but I know that you are good. I trust you to care for me and my family in the way that you see fit. You are a good Father. Thank you for your direction in my life. Give me a willing heart to follow.
In Jesus' Name, Amen

DAY 22

And we know that all things work together for good to those who love God, to those who are the called according to His purpose.
Romans 8:28 NKJV

Sometimes I wonder what the future will hold for my children, and it's honestly kind of scary. I often wish there was a way I could save them from experiencing heartache or sadness or sickness. I want to make sure they are happy, healthy, and fulfilled in life.

But it's an inescapable fact of life that I cannot protect them from everything. They will face hard things as they grow up and experience the world for themselves. They will go through seasons that I will want to pluck them out of. If not for my hope in Jesus Christ, this would be absolutely terrifying.

My children's futures may be unknown, but I know who holds their futures. I know that the Father loves them deeply – even more than I do – and is intimately involved in every aspect of their lives. And I know that He works all things together for good to those who love Him.

Now, that doesn't mean He works all things together to *be* good. At least not in a way that our finite human brains can fathom. He doesn't provide an easy or struggle-free life for His children, as much as I would like that guarantee as a mother.

However, He does work all things together *for* good. Maybe things won't always feel good or seem good in my life or in the lives of my children. But we have hope because we love the Lord. We know that His ultimate plan is unfolding through every circumstance we face, and we know that His plan is good.

Even if certain things never make sense on this side of heaven, we can rest assured that God is working. Even in our sickness, even in our pain, even in our sadness. He is never far from us, and He is never far from our children.

He loves them and cares for them even more than we do, and that is the absolute most comforting truth.

Lord Jesus, thank you that you work all things together for my good. I love you and I trust you, even when things are hard. I know that your plan is unfolding in my life, and that it is part of a bigger picture. Please comfort me in knowing that you love my children so deeply and so intimately. They are never beyond your care. I entrust their futures to you.
In Jesus' Name, Amen

DAY 23

"When you pass through the waters, I will be with you; and through the rivers, they shall not overflow you. When you walk through the fire, you shall not be burned, nor shall the flame scorch you."
Isaiah 43:2 NKJV

This verse doesn't say *if* you pass through the waters. It says *when* you pass through the waters.

That's because struggle and hardship are facts of life. There is no avoiding or escaping them. We *will* face hard things. We *will* go through tough seasons. That's a guarantee.

But it's also a guarantee that God will be with us through every single thing we face, no matter the waters we traverse, no matter the fires we must walk through. He will be with us every single step of the way, no questions asked.

So when we face seasons of struggle with our children, we shouldn't despair. When things get hard as a mom – little everyday things or big life-changing things – we can trust that He will be right there beside us, and He will bring us through.

Sometimes as mothers we feel broken, desperate, and helpless. We feel alone and afraid. But we are never too far from the Lord to cry out for His help. His hand is constantly holding us and our families. We can trust Him to lead us through whatever life brings our way.

When we promise to be there for our children, they trust us because they know we mean it wholeheartedly. How much more can we trust God's promises to us? He says He will be with us always, and we know He keeps His promises.

His plan will always prevail, so we can rest in that assurance, knowing that we are secure in His love.

Heavenly Father, thank you for your precious promise to never leave me. Whatever I face today, I know that you are with me. I trust you to care for me and my family. I know that your plans are good. You are a good Father, and I am your child. Thank you for calling me your own.
In Jesus' Name, Amen

DAY 24

He has made everything beautiful in its time.
Ecclesiastes 3:11a NIV

I get sad sometimes because my children are growing so fast. Every time I get comfortable with the phase we're in, everything changes again. It seems like yesterday my kids were in diapers, and now they're almost as tall as I am.

Where does the time go, and why does it have to fly by so quickly? I want to pause every moment and bottle it up so I can treasure it forever. But life doesn't work that way. Time marches on relentlessly, no matter how hard I try to hold on.

As bittersweet as it can be watching your kids grow up, there is such beauty in every season. Isn't it such a blessing to witness their personalities blossom before your eyes? Isn't it wonderful getting to watch them become the people God created them to be? As much as I want them to stay little, I also can't wait to see who they will be when they grow up.

God's design is absolutely perfect. He ordains every single day, every hour, every moment of our lives. And He is just as present and active in the lives of our children. Isn't that amazing?

Equally amazing is the fact that He has a purpose for every season in our family's lives. The joyful, the sad, the tiring – they are all part of His plan.

Each little stage my children go through teaches me something new. You see, it's not just about them growing up; it's about me growing too. Growing in grace, growing in love, growing in faith. Being a mother has given me more opportunities for growth than anything else in my life.

Whether you're in the diaper stage, the empty nest stage, or somewhere in between, God has a purpose for this chapter in your life. He is molding you day by day into the woman He wants you to be. And no matter what age your children are, He's working in their lives too.

Let that be the thought your heart dwells on today, and make it the focus of your prayers.

Lord Jesus, thank you so much for the gift of motherhood. Each season is unique and challenging but so very beautiful. I am so grateful for the children you have blessed me with. Help me to cherish each moment with them, and shape me into the woman you want me to be. Thank you for the growth you have allowed me to experience. Thank you for every wonderful chapter.
In Jesus' Name, Amen

DAY 25

"Fear not, for I am with you; be not dismayed, for I am your God. I will strengthen you, Yes, I will help you, I will uphold you with my righteous right hand."
Isaiah 41:10 NKJV

I know I've already said this several times, but it's something I really want you to remember: God is *always* with you.

I don't know about you, but it's easy for me to be afraid, especially as a mom. I want so badly to make sure that everything is okay. I put so much pressure on myself to take care of everyone and everything, and I stress or worry when things are beyond my control. I don't like it when there's not an easy answer to something, and I like it even less when there's nothing I can do to fix things.

Being a mom is scary and it's hard. I will never judge anyone for having anxiety or fear because I've been there so many times. I'm right there in the trenches, time and time again, fighting against anything that threatens the peace of my family. Overthinking and stressing and fretting to make sure everything is okay.

But here's the thing. We don't have to fight all those battles. We don't have to find all those answers. We don't have to make sure everything is okay. Most importantly, we don't have to be afraid.

In fact, God tells us *not* to be afraid. Is that because He promises that everything will go smoothly and we'll never have anything to worry about? Not at all. But He does promise to be with us and to strengthen us. He promises to uphold us and help us in our times of need.

If you're like me, you probably find something new to worry about every day. I get it, trust me. But I also know that there's so much freedom in surrendering those worries to God. Let Him have them. He can figure it out better than you ever could, and He's strong enough to shoulder your burdens.

Surrender your worries to Jesus. Banish fear from your heart and let His peace fill you instead. It's something you'll have to do repeatedly and with intention, but it's so simple and so very freeing.

Just give it all to Him.

Dear God, please strengthen me and uphold me today. Lord, there's so much on my mind and I can't handle it all on my own. I need your peace and your joy. Please help me to banish worry and fear from my heart. I choose to trust you instead.
In Jesus' Name, Amen

Perfect Peace

DAY 26

Let the peace of Christ rule in your hearts, since as members of one body you were called to peace. And be thankful.
Colossians 3:15 NIV

Peace and thankfulness go hand in hand. A heart with a posture of gratitude is generally more peaceful and content, whereas a heart lacking gratitude will tend to be more restless.

I worry a lot. It's a weakness I've struggled with for years, and I'm sure it'll continue to be a thorn in my flesh into the future. I do my best to fight it with Scripture and prayer, but there are days when I wake up and instantly start worrying. It's like a tidal wave that crashes into me as soon as my eyes open in the morning, robbing my entire day of peace and allowing an inner feeling of chaos to ensue.

Maybe you've had those days, and maybe it's a common occurrence for you like it is for me. It seems like there is always something for me to be stressed about. My brain finds any imperfection and obsesses over it until I can't think about anything else, and being a mom makes it ten times harder to resist because now I have little people to care for, which causes my anxiety to be even greater.

But do you know what I've found to be the best cure for this crippling anxiety? Thankfulness.

When I'm overwhelmed with worry and fear, I have a choice to make. I can let that fear consume me, or I can change my thinking. And what I've discovered is this: When I carve out time to spend with the Lord, actively thanking Him for everything I can possibly name, my anxiety fades away.

My strategy is to go for a walk (without my phone or any other distractions) and simply pour out my thanks to God. I thank Him for everything under the sun – whatever pops into my head. Before long I'm thanking Him for things I never thought to be grateful for.

This sets the tone for the rest of my day and helps me focus my mind on things above. Yes, there are things to worry about. Yes, my family is depending on me to take care of them, and that is a lot of responsibility. But there is also so much to be thankful for!

Choosing to focus on gratitude does wonders because it ushers in peace instead of anxiety, and that's the best medicine for my heart.

Lord Jesus, please uproot my destructive ways of thinking and replace them with your peace. Help me to focus my mind on thankfulness so peace can rule my heart. Forgive me for the times when I fail to be grateful. Lord, your blessings are all around me. You have been so good to me. I am in awe of your love.
In Jesus' Name, Amen

DAY 27

Depart from evil and do good; seek peace and pursue it.
Psalm 34:14 NKJV

Peace doesn't just happen on its own. The natural state of the world is chaos and disorder. That's not how God designed it, but the existence of sin has caused His perfect design to go astray.

In the same way, our homes are not magically peaceful. It's something we have to work toward. There are certain practices we have to uphold if we want to keep order. We have to form habits that cultivate a peaceful environment for our families to live in.

We must constantly pursue peace, and the first step in this is to be constantly pursuing Jesus. The most important thing we can do to ensure a peaceful home is to devote daily time to the Bible. We cannot be filled with the Spirit if we are not filled with God's Word. It's more than just a book full of words; it's a source of life and hope and peace. It's where we derive our joy and deepen our faith by growing closer to the Lord every day.

Pursuing peace means putting aside distractions, laying down idols, and choosing to put Jesus first. Our children are watching us, and they will see what takes up most of our time. They'll see our priorities and what's important to us. Will they see us pursuing Jesus, or are we too busy pursuing something else?

There's always something tempting us away from the Lord. Whether it's our fleshly desires, the devil's lies, peer pressure from other women, or the deadly comparison game, there's always something threatening to destroy our peace. That's why we must constantly seek peace. We must actively choose Jesus over everything else.

He doesn't give to us as the world gives. He gives life to the fullest, and that means an abundance of peace. He's offering that peace to us with open arms, but it's up to us to reach out and take it. We must choose to receive the gift, and then we must maintain it.

The peace in our homes begins with us. If we are not promoting an environment of peace, the rest of the family has no reason to do so either.

If you want your home to be a peaceful place, then make sure your heart is peaceful too.

Precious Jesus, thank you for the gift of peace. Help me to take hold of that gift and allow it to take root in my heart. Please banish all temptations and distractions my heart wants to cling to and help me to focus on you. You are the Prince of Peace. I am yours, now and forever, and I choose to dwell in your peace. In Jesus' Name, Amen

DAY 28

You will keep in perfect peace those whose minds are steadfast, because they trust in you.
Isaiah 26:3 NIV

Much like we talked about yesterday, God freely offers us peace. It's not conditional or something we have to earn. It's a free gift He graciously bestows upon us.

But like I said before, we have to choose to accept that gift. It's our job to trust Him and keep our minds steadfast. His peace is there for the taking, but He won't choose our thoughts for us. He doesn't force us to rest in that peace.

Is your mind cycling through worries about your family's future? Are you stressed because of all the events and dates on your calendar? Are you weak and weary because you haven't had a good night's sleep in who-knows-how-long?

That's normal. It's the way human brains work. Our minds are not naturally God-centered; they're naturally self-centered. Making them God-centered takes a lot of time, patience, and dedication.

A steadfast mind is not ruled by feelings. It is not swayed by the opinions of others. It is not easily upset by unforeseen difficulties. A steadfast mind is one that hopes in the Lord, even when things are tough. One that trusts that He has things under control, even when the situation feels downright impossible. Believes beyond a shadow of a doubt that He will provide.

It takes a lot of practice to have a steadfast mind. I don't know if it's totally achievable until we receive our glorified bodies, but the more we work toward having that state of mind, the more we feel rested and at peace.

Lots of things disrupt our peace as mothers. If I tried to make a list, it would take up the rest of this book. But no matter what it is that threatens to steal our peace, it doesn't surprise God. It doesn't make Him blink. He isn't fazed by anything.

He knows exactly how we feel and exactly what we need. He's with us. He's got it under control. All we have to do is trust Him and rest in His perfect peace.

Gracious Father, I need your peace more than I need oxygen. Sometimes I feel so lost and out of control, but I know that you are with me. Help my mind to be steadfast. Let your perfect peace fill my soul. Whatever comes, I know that you've got it handled. I trust you, Lord.
In Jesus' Name, Amen

DAY 29

"Peace I leave with you, My peace I give to you; not as the world gives do I give to you. Let not your heart be troubled, neither let it be afraid."
John 14:27 NKJV

I am honestly baffled by the fact that some people walk through life without the Lord. Seriously, how do they survive it? Especially with the responsibility of raising tiny humans, I regularly find myself on my knees, pleading for His strength.

The world tries to sell all sorts of self-help advice. Whether it's diet restrictions or opinions on school options or debates about vaccines, there's always something the world tries to tell you you're doing wrong. It's easy in this day and age to feel like a failure of a parent because we are so inundated with other people's opinions on what the "right way" is.

Stop listening to them! Stop getting your advice from people whose truth consists of nothing more than their feelings. Stop feeling guilty because some lady on Instagram parents differently than you. Your guidebook should be the Holy Bible, period.

Yes, we should seek wise counsel on certain things regarding our children. Of course, we should do all that we can to make sure they are healthy and well cared for. But we must stop listening to what the world thinks makes a good parent, and listen instead to the still small voice.

Have you ever wondered why God speaks in a still small voice when everyone else is yelling? It's because He's not trying to prove anything. He doesn't have anything to gain by convincing us He's right. He simply loves us and wants us to have true peace and joy.

When we parent the way God calls us to, chances are it'll clash with everything the world wants us to do. But we can walk in obedience to the Lord peacefully and unashamed because He promises to be faithful to His children.

Even if we're alone on the path we choose, we don't have to be afraid because we're never truly alone.

Let not your heart be troubled. Obedience to the Lord is so much better than fitting in with the world. Nothing the world offers will bring you true and lasting peace. Only Jesus can do that.

Heavenly Father, thank you for your perfect peace. You are nothing like the world, so I don't want to be either. Help me to pursue the peace that comes from obedience to you. Forgive me for falling prey to the enemy's lies and for striving to fit in. I want to look less like the world and more like you. I am unashamed to be your child.

In Jesus' Name, Amen

DAY 30

Finally, brothers and sisters, whatever is true, whatever is noble, whatever is right, whatever is pure, whatever is lovely, whatever is admirable—if anything is excellent or praiseworthy—think about such things.
Philippians 4:8 NIV

I must confess that I tend to focus on negative things more than positive things. Not only that, but I speak negatively in front of my children more than I should. They often hear me grumbling and complaining, when I should be an example to them of hope and joy.

There's a lot of bad stuff going on in the world, and it can be tempting to place our focus on all the negativity. But isn't it so much more peaceful and healthy for our families when we focus on the good things? Everyone feels lighter and fresher when their minds are occupied with things that are lovely and excellent and praiseworthy.

As mothers, it is our duty not to become a source of stress or anxiety for young minds that can't fully understand mature subjects. Instead, we are called to protect them and provide them with peace. It's up to us to guard their hearts until they're old enough to guard them on their own.

It's a big task for sure. One that sometimes feels insurmountable. Especially when kids are bombarded from every direction these days. No matter where you turn, there's someone or something threatening to chip away at their innocence.

We can't possibly prevent our kids from encountering every single ugly or nasty thing, but we can make sure that our homes are places of peace. And that starts with a conscious decision on our parts to focus on things that are good, noble, right, and pure. Because our thinking becomes our speaking, and our speaking becomes our doing.

If we want to act in a peaceful manner and speak in a peaceful manner, we must first train our minds to think in a peaceful manner. Peace isn't found in fretting or worrying. It's not found in gossiping. It's not found in grumbling or arguing. And it's certainly not found in tearing others down.

It's found in a mind that runs back to Jesus every single time it starts to wander and a heart that's filled with His goodness, leaving room for nothing else.

Heavenly Father, please help me train my mind to focus on the good. Help me to think about things that are lovely and noble and excellent and praiseworthy. Forgive me for my grumbling and my negativity. I know that peace is found in a mind that is focused on you. Help me to spread that peace to my family and set a positive example. Thank you for your grace and your mercy.

In Jesus' Name, Amen

Soak up the Son

DAY 31

Your word I have hidden in my heart, that I might not sin against you.
Psalm 119:11 NKJV

We must be filled with the Word in order to live it, and we need to live it in order to love our families well.

How can we possibly expect ourselves to act in a Christlike manner if we're not filling ourselves with Christ? No one would try to pass the Bar Exam without cracking open a law textbook, nor would you try to become a doctor without going to medical school. So it stands to reason that we aren't fully equipped to live out the Christian life if we're not well versed in God's Word.

I know it's hard to find time alone, especially if your children are young and extremely dependent. Sometimes it's all you can do to make it through the day and sneak in a five-minute shower. There's not a lot of quiet time or free time, or really any extra time at all.

But you *need* to find time to devote to Jesus. You've got to make time for the Bible. It's imperative for your spiritual health, and it's crucial for the well-being of your family. I promise that it will make a big difference, even if you only have ten minutes to spare. Give what you can to Him, and watch what He can do with it.

I didn't start reading the Bible daily until my second child was born. I knew I needed to have that lifeblood flowing through my veins, so I made a commitment to reading the Bible all the way through in a year.

I ended up completing it in ten months because I found I couldn't get enough. Once I made the habit of reading for fifteen minutes every day, it became like second nature. My day no longer felt complete unless I spent time in the Word.

My son is almost eight years old now, and I haven't stopped giving daily time to God's Word. Let me tell you, I wish I had started much sooner! It really has deepened my walk with God in so many ways, and I believe it has opened the door for spiritual growth for my children as well.

When you hide God's Word in your heart, you're doing more than just reading a book. You're infusing your soul with life-giving words and fueling your spiritual health, and that will have a profound impact on those around you, starting with your family.

Gracious Lord, thank you for your Word. Thank you that it is alive and active and mine for the taking. Forgive me for the times when I've neglected to spend time with you. Help me to fall deeper in love with your Word and hide it in my heart. Please let me be a fountain of wisdom and love and joy, overflowing with your grace as I care for my family.
In Jesus's Name, Amen

DAY 32

"We do not know what to do, but our eyes are on you."
2 Chronicles 20:12b NIV

Being a mother has tested me more than anything else in my life. There are a lot of times when I just don't know what to do. Situations arise that I've never faced before and have no idea how to handle, and I often question whether I'm doing it all wrong or failing somehow. What if I mess my kids up?

Have you ever felt that way? Like you're in over your head? Like you're doing your best but have no idea what the right answer is?

It's okay to feel that way. You're not supposed to figure it all out on your own. You're not supposed to have all the answers. That's God's job. You're just supposed to keep your eyes on Him.

Those times when we don't know what to do are actually gifts, because they're opportunities for us to trust Him. It gives us the chance to grow our faith because we have to loosen our grip and relinquish control. Maybe we don't know what to do, but we can trust that He always knows what to do.

If you read the entire chapter of 2 Chronicles 20, the situation looked hopeless. The people of Judah were in big trouble, and their outlook was pretty bleak. Armies surrounded them on every side, ready to attack with all their might.

But King Jehoshaphat didn't look to his own strength or seek out human wisdom. He turned to the Lord in a desperate plea for help. He admitted that he was powerless and needed God's wisdom and strength.

The next day, the Lord came through in a way that no one ever could have expected. He delivered His people without them even lifting a finger. He provided for them and protected them, in His perfect timing and in His mighty way.

If you don't know what to do, look to Him. Admit that you're lost and in need of guidance. Ask Him for clarity. Seek His strength. Allow Him to fight on your behalf.

Keep your eyes on Him and watch Him work in mighty ways.

Holy Lord, I don't know what to do, but my eyes are on you. I need your guidance and your wisdom and your strength. Just as you rescued Jehoshaphat and the people of Judah, fight on behalf of my family. I trust you, Lord. Only you can deliver me.
My eyes are on you.
In Jesus' Name, Amen

DAY 33

But those who wait on the Lord shall renew their strength; they shall mount up with wings like eagles, they shall run and not be weary, they shall walk and not faint.
Isaiah 40:31 NKJV

I don't know your story, but I'm guessing you're under a lot of pressure. Whether you're a stay-at-home mom, a working mom, a work-from-home mom, or a homeschool mom, there's always enormous pressure. None of these situations are easy, and they all come with their challenges.

If you ever feel like you're carrying the weight of the world on your shoulders, you're not alone. I think we've all felt that way at some point. Maybe you've convinced yourself that providing everything your family needs falls completely on your shoulders. Maybe you're paralyzed and crushed by the mountain of responsibility that comes with being a mom.

But you don't have to carry that burden. You can give it to Jesus and let Him carry it for you.

Let Him carry your family. Let Him sustain you. He never grows weary or runs out of strength. His arms have enough room for you and your family and everything that keeps you awake at night. There's nothing He can't handle. Nothing is too big or too small for Him to care about.

When you seek the Lord with all your heart, He will give you the strength and sustenance you need. He will recharge and revitalize you to face the day ahead.

Remember from the Lord's Prayer (Matthew 6:9-13) that we are to ask for our daily bread. Not tomorrow's bread, but today's. Lean on the Lord as you focus on today. Not what's up ahead, but the task before you right now. Seek Him and watch as your strength is renewed.

Soaring on wings like eagles sounds a lot better than sinking in a pit of despair, doesn't it? I would much rather walk and not faint than try to carry a backbreaking load.

He never designed us to wade through the waters alone. He intended us to keep our eyes fixed on Him and forget about the oncoming waves. He wants to carry us, but we have to be willing to let Him.

God Almighty, I need your strength today. Help me to trust in you and allow you to renew my strength. Lord, I want to mount up with wings like eagles. I want to run and not grow weary. Refresh my spirit and breathe your life into me. Give me this day my daily bread. Lord, you are strong enough for the both of us. I put my faith in you.
In Jesus' Name, Amen

DAY 34

"Come to me, all you who are weary and burdened, and I will give you rest."
Matthew 11:28 NIV

Being a mom is exhausting. There's no delicate way to put it.

When little people have total dependency on you 24 hours a day, it starts to take a toll on your energy. Not just the baby phase, although that is definitely draining with the lack of sleep, but every season of parenting. As rewarding and beautiful as it is, nothing in life wears you out quite like being a mother.

We mamas are tired. We need rest. Sleep, yes. Time to relax and unwind, yes. But most of all, we need spiritual rest. That's the rest we need more than precious sleep, more than reading a book or watching a movie, more than sitting down to drink a cup of coffee while it's still hot.

The most beneficial form of rest is laying our burdens at the feet of our Savior and letting Him carry our load. When we're weary and burnt out and not sure how to carry on, we can fall into His arms. We can burrow into His tender love and mercy and let the Spirit fill our souls. When we're at the end of our rope, that's where we find His strength takes us even further. It's such a beautiful and freeing thing to let Him have our burdens.

No amount of sleep or relaxation could ever recharge or revitalize us quite like time spent in the presence of Jesus. Not that those things aren't needed too, but the rest we find in Jesus is the only rest that allows us to truly feel at peace. Our hearts yearn for His presence, and our bodies feel the difference when we properly feed our souls.

It's hard to pull out that Bible when you're exhausted. It's difficult to utter a prayer when you're weary. But when you reach out to Jesus – when you seek Him and put your focus on Him – He refills your soul with lifegiving power that overflows into every aspect of your life.

If you're feeling weary or burdened today, give it to Jesus. Lie down in the green pastures and beside the still waters. Let your soul find rest.

Lord Jesus, I am weary and burdened. I need your rest. Lord, fill me with your presence and surround me with your peace. You are all I need. My soul longs for you. Without you, I would fall apart. Lord, thank you for the rest you give.
In Jesus' Name, Amen

DAY 35

"But seek first the kingdom of God and His righteousness, and all these things shall be added to you."
Matthew 6:33 NKJV

Do you have a never-ending to-do list? Because I know I do. Seriously. I have sticky notes all over my planner and my desk with various lists of things that need to be done within various amounts of time. It feels great crossing things off those lists, but then I add a bunch more and feel like I'm starting all over again.

It seems like there's always something I need to be doing. And if I'm not doing something, I feel like I *should* be doing something. And still, no matter what I do or how productive I am, I somehow always feel guilty for not doing something else. Like if I work too much, I feel bad for not spending more time with my kids. But then I feel bad for not working more on the days where I decide to have fun.

I also get overwhelmed by the constant need that comes along with parenting. I have to make sure everyone has clean clothes to wear every week. I have to plan out and cook three meals a day, and coming up with things that everyone is pleased with can be tough, plus all the cleanup that comes along with that. Not only that, but there are doctor's visits, grocery trips, oil changes, and various other errands to schedule and execute.

Sometimes I get so caught up in everything my family needs that I forget what we need most of all. It's not something I have to stress over or pencil into my planner. It's not something I can buy in a store or order off the internet. And it's not something I can work toward or achieve if I just strive to be productive.

No, what my family needs most of all is Jesus, plain and simple. He's what *I* need most of all, too. If I seek Him first and make Him my number-one priority, all the rest will fall into place in His timing, so I can let go and trust that He's got it under control.

He wants my heart. Not my carefully crafted schedule or my abundance of crossed-out sticky notes. He doesn't want piles of folded laundry or a sparkly clean kitchen. Those things are great, but He just wants me. And I don't have to do any extra work to give myself to Him. What a blessing!

If you're overwhelmed by all the things your family needs and all the work ahead of you today, take a moment to just breathe. Close your eyes and picture Jesus holding you in His arms, working everything together with His loving touch.

He's all you need. Give yourself to Him, and let Him take care of the rest.

Lord Jesus, I seek you first. You are all I need. You are enough for me. Please provide for me and my family and keep us safe from harm. Thank you for your providence and protection. I trust your timing and your plan, and I entrust my heart to you. You alone are God. I am in awe of you.
In Jesus' Name, Amen

Forgive and Be Forgiven

DAY 36

And be kind to one another, tenderhearted, forgiving one another, even as God in Christ forgave you.
Ephesians 4:32 NKJV

There are times when I get overwhelmed by the amazing fact that Jesus died for me. When I really stop to think about it, it moves me to tears. I'm so unworthy and so undeserving of His mercy and His grace, yet He loves me so much that He came to earth as a little baby, endured life in a human body, then suffered and died for me. All so that I could one day spend forever with Him? It's unfathomable.

He is the ultimate and perfect example of forgiveness. If there was a picture in the dictionary next to the word *forgive*, I think that spot would be given to our Lord. He does it best, bar none. He is the greatest picture of sacrificial love the world has ever known, and nothing could ever compare.

It's that picture and that example that I want to live out for my family. Because, let's be honest, sometimes forgiveness is hard. Really hard. Probably one of the hardest things to do because it doesn't always feel fair.

But that's exactly the point. It's not fair. We didn't deserve what Jesus did for us on the cross. We don't deserve His mercies that are new every morning. We don't deserve a single ounce of His love or care, and yet He freely bestows it upon us as soon as we call on His name. So who are we to withhold that from others?

Forgiveness doesn't mean you allow someone to continue in destructive behavior. It doesn't mean you don't speak up or offer gentle correction. Forgiveness isn't a free pass or a get-out-of-jail-free card.

It's a conscious decision to continue loving someone without holding a grievance against them. Maybe sometimes that means loving them prayerfully from afar, but it's important that our children see us making the choice to forgive. Choosing not to hold a grudge or allow bitterness to take root, but having a heart of forgiveness instead. Even – and maybe especially – when it's hard.

Forgiveness is a Christlike attribute, and it's one we should all strive to emulate. If we want to look more like Jesus, we must be sure our hearts are willing to forgive.

After all, if the perfect and spotless Lamb could love me enough to take my place on the cross, it's the least I can do to forgive my fellow, sinful human.

Gracious Lord Jesus, thank you so much for the gift of forgiveness. Thank you for showing me what it means to forgive. Lord, I am so undeserving of your mercy and grace, yet you pour it out for me every single day. God, you are so good. Help me to extend forgiveness to others, just as you have done for me. Let no bitterness take root in my heart, and help me set a good example for my children.

In Jesus' Name, Amen

DAY 37

Bear with each other and forgive one another if any of you has a grievance against someone. Forgive as the Lord forgave you.
Colossians 3:13 NIV

Today's verse tells us to bear with each other, but what does that mean? Well, we're all imperfect humans with growing and learning yet to do. Bearing with one another means to be patient and tolerate each other's mistakes while we grow. Patience is really the key here. Extending grace because we realize that nobody is perfect and we all mess up sometimes.

This is something our children especially need from us, but it's easy to forget that our kids are human, too. We expect them to always be cooperative and obey immediately every time. We forget that they have bad days just like we do, and we fail to realize that they're facing so many things for the first time. They're learning and growing so much. We have to be willing to give them grace.

As a mother, you have the unique opportunity to model forgiveness for your children. Just as the Lord forgives you, you can forgive your children when they make the wrong choice. Just as Jesus bears with you patiently and gently, you can bear with your children as they figure out this thing called life.

Discipline is important, of course, and there are certain behaviors we simply cannot allow. But there are also times for gentle instruction, where we can demonstrate forbearance and grace. We can talk through situations and choices our children are presented with, and we can be their safe place when they mess up. Because they *will* mess up. That's something we can't avoid.

When that happens, though, we can demonstrate a balance of grace and discipline. This is one reason we need to spend time in prayer and studying the Word – so we can have discernment in these tough moments with our kids. They're watching how we respond, and our extending or withholding of forgiveness matters.

In any tough situation with our children, we must ask ourselves, "How would Christ respond?" And then we must do our best to act accordingly.

Father God, help me to extend forgiveness to my children, just as you have done for me. Lord, help me not to lack discipline, but help me also not to lack grace. Give me discernment and help me to find the right balance. Thank you for my children. Thank you that we get to learn and grow together. Forgive me for my shortcomings, and help me to be more like you.
In Jesus' Name, Amen

DAY 38

"For if you forgive other people when they sin against you, your heavenly Father will also forgive you. But if you do not forgive others their sins, your Father will not forgive your sins."
Matthew 6:14-15 NIV

Have you ever been deeply hurt by someone? So much so that you felt you could never move on? I know I've been there. It's not a good feeling at all, and it's hard to let go of that pain and anger. It's easier to hold onto resentment and bitterness.

People don't always deserve our forgiveness, but the truth is that none of us deserve forgiveness at all. We don't deserve God's grace or His mercy or His unconditional love. We are so far from being worthy of His amazing grace, yet He pours it out on us anyway.

God's forgiveness isn't based on merit, so ours shouldn't be either. We shouldn't forgive someone just because we feel they deserve it. No, we should extend forgiveness freely because it's what Christ modeled for us. Even though it's hard. Even though it hurts. Even though letting go doesn't erase our pain. But it's what He calls us to do.

And that's a very important thing to teach our children, no matter their age. They're never too young to learn about forgiveness – both seeking it when needed *and* extending it to others.

Another concept that goes hand in hand with this is apologizing. Too many parents never apologize to their children, and that's not healthy. There's this idea that the parent is always right that I just can't get behind. Yes, the parent is the authority and children are called to obedience, but that doesn't mean that parents never make mistakes. It doesn't mean we're incapable of hurting our children.

We say things we don't mean and we do the wrong thing sometimes, so sometimes we need to humble ourselves and confess that we were wrong. We need to acknowledge our failings and apologize for them. This gives our children a healthy way to exercise the act of forgiveness, and it's healing for their little hearts when their hurts are validated.

Forgiveness is a two-way street, even with children. Never be afraid to seek your children's forgiveness.

Precious Savior, I praise you for your amazing grace.
Thank you for forgiving me, a sinner so undeserving.
Help me to have a heart of forgiveness toward people who have hurt me. Help me also to seek forgiveness when I've hurt someone else, including my children.
Lord, I want to follow your ways.
I want to forgive and be forgiven.
In Jesus' Name, Amen

DAY 39

If we say that we have no sin, we deceive ourselves, and the truth is not in us. If we confess our sins, He is faithful and just to forgive us our sins and to cleanse us from all unrighteousness.
1 John 1:8-9 NKJV

I addressed this yesterday, but I think it's so important that it's worth talking about again. Parents are not above reproach. If you think you don't need correction or reproof every now and then, you're deceiving yourself.

The truth is that we are all inclined toward sin. Being a mother doesn't take that sin nature away from you. No matter how old you are or how many kids you have, you will never attain perfection. You will never stop making mistakes. Maybe they'll be fewer and farther between, but they'll still be there.

When our kids come to us and tell us we've hurt them, it's vital that we listen and receive it well. Even if we feel shocked, even if their confession pierces our heart, we must never make them feel bad for being honest with us.

We have to take ownership of our own behavior and the way we've made them feel. We absolutely must be willing to listen to their side of the story with an understanding and gentle heart. And then we must swallow our pride and apologize for our wrongs.

It's hard, I know. My kids are still young, but I've already experienced this several times. It's not easy to realize that you've caused your baby pain. It's difficult to lay down your pride and take responsibility for your behavior. But we have to do it. The health of our relationships with our kids depends on it. If we want to have close relationships with them into adulthood, they have to know they can trust us.

Let us not deceive ourselves into thinking we're without sin. That's utter foolishness and absolutely not pleasing to God.

But He is faithful and just. He is willing to forgive our iniquities. All we have to do is turn to Him and confess. A heart of repentance is sweeter than honey to Him. He will never turn us away.

Gracious Lord Jesus, I know I've failed you in so many ways. I know I fail my children sometimes, too. I'm not perfect, Lord. Only you are. Help me to have a heart of repentance. Never let me be too prideful to admit I was wrong and seek forgiveness. Help my children to know they can come to me with anything. Thank you for cleansing me from all unrighteousness. In Jesus' Name, Amen

DAY 40

Produce fruit in keeping with repentance.
Matthew 3:8 NIV

From a young age, kids are taught to say sorry. Even toddlers at the playground are encouraged to apologize when they accidentally hurt someone or take a toy away from their playmate. Being able to apologize is something we all want to instill in our children.

But just saying sorry isn't enough. Sorry is merely an empty word if it's not accompanied by action. If someone is really sorry, then they will make an effort to change. Of course, this is difficult to teach to toddlers, but it's something we can model for children of any age, and we can guide them as they learn to put it into practice.

If an apology is to be meaningful, it must come from a heart of repentance. It's not something we say just so someone won't be mad at us anymore. It's not a blanket statement we use to placate someone we've wronged, whether it was intentional or not.

True repentance requires a change of heart and an effort to do better. I like to read the Psalms written by David because he's such a beautiful example of this. He wasn't special because he never did anything wrong or messed up. He made plenty of mistakes and made his own share of bad choices. But he was set apart because he displayed remorse over his wrongdoing. He didn't shrug his shoulders and say *oh well.* He truly cared about the fact that he'd failed to measure up, and he repented of his sin wholeheartedly.

As we work to embody forgiveness with our children, let us remember to also embody repentance. Both are crucial pieces in maintaining a heart of praise. If our hearts are not in a posture of repentance, it will be hard to forgive. And on the flip side, if we aren't willing to forgive, we'll probably struggle to repent.

Forgiveness and repentance work together like a well-oiled machine. One cannot exist without the other, so we must bear fruit in both areas.

Heavenly Father, help me to bear fruit in keeping with repentance. Help me to demonstrate true repentance for my children. Gracious Lord, thank you for your grace when I fall short. Help me to turn from my flesh and walk in your Spirit. Create in me a pure heart and guide me in the truth. I am yours, now and forever.
In Jesus' Name, Amen

Stand Firm

DAY 41

Be on your guard; stand firm in the faith; be courageous; be strong.
1 Corinthians 16:13 NIV

This world is not an easy place to live in, and it's not getting any easier. In fact, it's getting more and more hostile toward people of faith. Whether that's indicative of the impending end times or not, we still have to endure until Jesus returns to take us home.

It seems like Christians are gradually being marginalized in our society today. We're under attack more than ever before. Maybe we don't personally experience persecution like our brothers and sisters do in other parts of the world, but the general attitude toward us is becoming more aggressive.

So what do we do? Do we shrink back and stay quiet? Do we bury our heads in the sand and hope to go unnoticed? To be honest, that's what I'd rather do.

But that's not what we're commanded to do. We're commanded to be courageous and strong and to stand firm in the faith. We are to be bold for the Lord, willing to stand for Him even if we stand alone. Jesus did not back down when He faced being tortured and murdered for our sake, so we mustn't back down when it comes time to defend His name.

Our families need to see us be brave. Our kids need our examples of boldness and courage in the face of ridicule. The future generation is counting on us to pave the way. If we don't stand firm, how can we expect our children to?

Of course, this doesn't mean we lash out with harsh words or argue with people just for the sake of it. We have to exercise discernment in every situation, considering whether we are casting our pearls before swine (Matthew 7:6). Sometimes it's best to hold our tongues, but sometimes we must speak up. If we don't, Luke 19:40 says that the rocks will cry out in our place. I don't know about you, but I don't want rocks to take my place in praising the Creator because I was too cowardly to do so myself.

Let your children witness your courage for Christ. Let them see that you care more about what God thinks than what people of the world might say. Stand firm in the faith so that your children will be emboldened to do the same.

Holy Father, enable me to stand firm in the faith. Give me your strength and conviction to hold fast to the end. Lord, don't let me shrink back in the face of persecution. Let my heart be stirred to action and my faith be bolder than ever. Help me to show my children what it means to be strong and courageous. In all things, let my life point to you.

In Jesus' Name, Amen

DAY 42

Blessed is the one who perseveres under trial because, having stood the test, that person will receive the crown of life that the Lord has promised to those who love him.
James 1:12 NIV

Does motherhood ever test your patience? If you answered no, you must be a saint. Because it tests mine almost every single day. Not only do my children push my buttons from time to time, but the sheer amount of responsibility that comes with parenting often feels overwhelming. I'm exhausted more than I'm not, and I usually can't wait to climb into bed at the end of the day.

There are trials that come with motherhood. There are really hard seasons. There are scary situations. There are tiring days and months and years. There are tears of worry and exhaustion and pain. There are days when we want to give up.

But we persevere. We continue on. We push through those tough days and hard seasons. We keep going when things are hard. When we're weak and weary, we rely on God's strength and the power of the Holy Spirit, and that's what gets us through.

Here's something beautiful we don't often realize in the midst of our struggles: Persevering doesn't just allow us to survive; it actually gives us life.

Every time we overcome an obstacle or weather a storm, we gain more confidence in God's sovereignty. Each time He brings us through a trial, our faith muscles are stretched and grown. Our joy becomes greater and our hope stronger when we witness His work in our lives. It takes those exhausting seasons and times of testing for us to fully rely on His strength.

When we rest in His arms and persevere by His grace, we deepen our relationship with Him. He breathes life into our souls when we allow Him to carry our burdens.

Perseverance is not some accomplishment we can ever achieve on our own. It's something we are enabled to do only when we surrender to God's plan and keep our eyes on Him. We don't worry about the storms because we know He's right there with us.

That knowledge is the sweetest knowledge anyone could ever have. It allows us to breathe easy and rest secure. We can have life to the fullest because we know who's in control.

Holy Lord, help me to persevere through the trials I'm facing. Give me the strength and energy I need to face this day. I am nothing without you, Lord. I need your freedom and your joy. I want your abundant peace and your everlasting hope. Thank you for never leaving me, no matter what I face. Thank you that I can live life to the fullest because I know you are in control.
In Jesus' Name, Amen

DAY 43

No discipline seems pleasant at the time, but painful. Later on, however, it produces a harvest of righteousness and peace for those who have been trained by it.
Hebrews 12:11 NIV

Discipline is hard. It doesn't matter if you're on the giving end or the receiving end – it's not an easy thing. But discipline is important for both us *and* our children.

We must be disciplined in our faith and in our daily habits. We must live in a state of surrender, not to our own fleshly desires, but to what glorifies our Heavenly Father. When we stray from the path we're meant to take, He often disciplines us because He is a loving Father who wants His children to go the right way. This looks different depending on each situation, but God invokes discipline when He needs to catch our attention or get us back on track.

In the same way, we must discipline our children. We don't do this to humiliate or oppress them, as some people in the world wrongly believe. It's not because we're authoritarian dictators who enjoy yelling at our kids.

We discipline our children because we love them. We want them to do what's right and become the people God created them to be. We want them to make wise choices and treat people well. Sometimes this requires correction, because our children are human and they make mistakes. They aren't born knowing how to behave. They have to be taught, and it's our responsibility to teach them.

It's not my place to suggest specific methods of discipline. That's between you and God. But I will remind you to keep Him in mind when you discipline your children. When anger and frustration threaten to boil over, take a moment to gather your thoughts and ask God for wisdom. Discipline is best administered calmly, not in the heat of the moment or out of anger.

As we discipline our children, though it feels difficult at the time, we are training them to deny the flesh and walk in the Spirit. And in doing so, we are helping produce a harvest of righteousness and peace in their lives.

Lord Jesus, thank you for your discipline in my life. I need your correction and guidance. Thank you for helping me choose what's right. Lord, help me to do the same for my children. Help me to discipline them out of love. I pray that my children would follow you all the days of their lives and enjoy a harvest of righteousness and peace.
Thank you for your many blessings.
In Jesus' Name, Amen

DAY 44

"But as for me and my house, we will serve the Lord."
Joshua 24:15b NKJV

Children don't just magically come to faith on their own. They need to be discipled and shepherded. We have to teach them who God is and why we follow Him.

Kids will be kids. They won't always want to go to church or read the Bible or pray. It's not human nature to desire those things. Thanks to the fall of man, we have to refine our souls to seek after the Lord. I mean, I'd rather sleep in than get up and have my quiet time, but I have to exercise self-discipline and do the right thing. So, of course, we have to instill heavenly values into our little ones, too.

Make it clear that serving God is a priority to your family and create boundaries that clearly express that. Whatever it might look like for your household, make it your mission to put God first in everything. Allow Him to take first priority in your home, and you'll be amazed at the changes that will occur.

Making Jesus the focus of your family will never make them less happy or less healthy or less fulfilled. It will only ever increase their joy, their well-being, and their fulfillment in life.

Make the declaration right now that your house will serve the Lord. Give Him this day and allow Him to work in your family. Put Him at the top of your priorities, and watch as that trickles down to your children. Watch them start to develop joy and pleasure in serving the Lord. It's such a beautiful thing to witness your kids putting Jesus first in their lives.

Yes, it might start as something routine and ordinary. But as they learn and grow in their relationships with God, their faith will bloom and flourish. They will start serving and praising the Lord because they *want* to – because it makes their hearts feel whole and secure.

A home that serves the Lord is a home filled with peace. Let your praise fill each room of your house, and let each day be a reason to worship.

Almighty God, I choose to serve you today. You are first and foremost in all things. Without you I am nothing. Let my praise be pleasing to your ears, and help me to set the example for my family of putting you first. Nothing else matters if you aren't at the heart of my home. I love you, Lord. Thank you for allowing me to serve you.
In Jesus' Name, Amen

DAY 45

Let us hold unswervingly to the hope we profess, for he who promised is faithful.
Hebrews 10:23 NIV

God is so faithful to us. In every season, He is good.

There are times when life feels anything but good, yet that doesn't change one single thing about God's character.

No matter what we face in this world, we can hold unswervingly to hope because we know that this world is not our home. He promised to take us to heaven to spend forever with Him, and we know that He is faithful to keep His promises.

When life throws us curveballs and fastballs and knocks us on our face, we can still hold onto hope. Nothing can take our hope away, not a single thing. And that's something we can encourage our families to hold onto as well.

The world will try to tell us that God doesn't care. It will laugh at us and mock us. It will try to shame us for believing in a good God. But we can stand firm because we know the truth. We can proclaim Jesus as Lord without wavering, without stumbling, without hiding in shame. He *is* Lord and He *is* King, whether the world acknowledges Him or not.

Our hope is not based on anything the world can offer. We don't hang our hat on flesh and blood, nor do we trust in any earthly treasure. Our hope is in Christ alone, for He alone can promise us a secure future. That's what we hold firm to, because we know that He is faithful.

Instill this hope into your children today. Make sure they know that this world will eventually let them down.

Nothing is guaranteed in this life. But we do have hope and a secure future in Christ, and that is what truly matters.

We will all one day pass from this life, but God's Word will never pass away. Praise be to God that He has granted us a way to spend eternity with Him. Let us hold unswervingly to the promise of life, because He who promised is faithful.

Gracious Heavenly Father, I know that you are faithful. Thank you for the hope you have given me and the gift of eternal life. Whatever this world brings, I know that my future is secure. My hope is in you, Lord. You are the Author and Perfector of my faith. You are the Rock on which I stand.
In Jesus' Name, Amen

Spread Kindness & Speak Life

DAY 46

For we are His workmanship, created in Christ Jesus for good works, which God prepared beforehand that we should walk in them.
Ephesians 2:10 NKJV

We are saved by grace alone, not any good works that we can do. No amount of hard work or acts of kindness can earn your way into heaven. Only accepting Jesus Christ as Lord and Savior will grant you eternal salvation.

But good works *are* important. God created us to do good things, to shine a light into this dark and desperate world. He wants us to spread kindness to those around us and be His hands and feet.

Good works are how we put God's love on full display. If our hearts are in a place of humility, with a genuine desire to serve others, then God ultimately gets all the glory.

We are His workmanship, which means that He designed us and created us and fashioned us in a certain way, and part of that design was for us to do good works. He actually prepared the opportunity for these works for us ahead of time. How awesome is that? So when these opportunities arise, I hope we are willing to step up and act.

This is also beautiful because it's something we can implement in our family time. Look for opportunities to help someone in need. Take time together to serve others. It doesn't have to be big and grand. Little acts of kindness go a long way, and you never know the impact your actions might have in someone's life. Get your kids involved and go spread some kindness. In blessing others, you will find yourself doubly blessed, and the smiles on your children's faces will be the icing on the cake.

When we act obediently in doing good works, we put God's majesty on display and show that we are part of His beautiful masterpiece. We were literally created for this function, so let's have joy in fulfilling our purpose!

Lord Jesus, thank you for creating me for good works. Help my eyes to be open to opportunities to spread kindness. Let me never be too busy to serve others or be kind. You have shown me the way, Lord. Help me to walk in it. Thank you for allowing me to be part of your masterpiece. You make such wonderful things.
In Jesus' Name, Amen

DAY 47

Who is wise and understanding among you? Let them show it by their good life, by deeds done in the humility that comes from wisdom.
James 3:13 NIV

Our goal, not only as mothers but as Christians in general, should be to make the gospel attractive. Pointing others to Jesus should be the desire of our hearts. We must be wise and understanding, displaying Christ through humility and acts of love.

A good life makes the gospel attractive. We won't win people to the kingdom by having big houses or stylish clothes or silky hair. It's not our outer appearance that truly shines; it's the Spirit dwelling inside of us and the joy that only comes from His presence.

Just as our outer adornment isn't what sets us apart, we certainly won't attract people to the kingdom if we're full of anger or pride or jealousy. If we want people to see Jesus in us, we have to bear fruit consistent with His character.

Kindness is important. Patience is key. Self-control is a must. And along with those, we must be humble and not self-serving. Our main priority should never be our own happiness. We should serve others gladly and wholeheartedly, as if we were serving the Lord.

This applies to our families as well. Whether our children already know the Lord or we're still praying for them to receive salvation, it's crucial for us to model a good life for them. Not a life that is good by worldly standards, but a life that radiates the gospel message. A life that shines for Jesus, even when we think no one is watching. Because I can guarantee that your children *are* watching.

Even if they're toddlers who can barely formulate a coherent sentence, they're watching. Even when they're teenagers who stare at their phones and roll their eyes at everything you say, they're watching. Even if they're grown up and out of the house, they're still watching.

The way you live your life matters. You are setting a standard for your children to live by. You are creating the roadmap that will set them on the course to their future. Are you living a life consistent with God's Word? Are you making the gospel attractive?

Let your focus today be on making small changes. Maybe it's a shift in mindset or a break from certain distractions. Consider what might help your life be better illuminated by Christ, and make a conscious effort to work toward that change.

Holy Lord, thank you for the gift of your Spirit. Help me to embody your love and kindness today. Let my life be a shining witness to your great love. Let the truth radiate from a life well lived. Thank you for the chance to be an example for my children. I pray that they see you when they look at me.
In Jesus' Name, Amen

DAY 48

Do not let any unwholesome talk come out of your mouths, but only what is helpful for building others up according to their needs, that it may benefit those who listen.
Ephesians 4:29 NIV

This verse has always been convicting to me, but even more so once I became a mother. Especially that last part: "That it may benefit those who listen." *Oof.* Who are the people listening to me the most? Yep, you guessed it. My kids. And I'm not sure I always like what they hear.

Listen, I know firsthand that controlling the mouth is a struggle. Nobody can totally tame their tongue and only speak kind words. Thinking about someone who could conjures an image of Snow White singing with little tweeting birds floating around her head. Nobody is that lovely and sweet all the time. Everybody says things they don't mean, and we all wish we could take back certain words we've spoken.

But the majority of the things we say should be wholesome and pure. We should be building others up, not tearing them down. *Yikes.* I know this is a problem for most women. It's easier to pick somebody apart than to lift them up, isn't it? It's a lot more interesting to gossip and talk about rumors than it is to pray for someone who's having a hard time. But none of that is glorifying to God, nor does it benefit those who listen.

We don't know people's stories. We don't see their struggles when no one else is around. There's only about 1 percent of their life that we're privy to, so it's not our place to speculate about the other 99 percent. It's not kind or Christlike to speak negatively about people all the time. And let's be honest, nobody likes a Negative Nancy. Chances are, if she's talking about everybody else *to* you, then she's probably talking *about* you too. Don't be that person!

Words are powerful. They can give someone hope and life, or they can plunge them into a pit of despair. Perhaps we don't have power to create things with just a word like God does, but we absolutely have power to hurt or heal with our words. I believe the things we say will matter in eternity, and that's not something we should take lightly.

Our words will either speak life or darkness to our families. Let them speak life!

Gracious Heavenly Father, please forgive me for my careless words. I'm sorry for all the times I've torn people down with the things I've said. Help me to speak life into people. Help my words to be a source of hope and encouragement. Lord, I want to love people the way you love them. Show me the way and guide me in your love.

In Jesus' Name, Amen

DAY 49

Even so the tongue is a little member and boasts great things. See how great a forest a little fire kindles!
James 3:5 NKJV

Our tongues are small but powerful. A single spark can start a flame, but will we start fires of love or fires of destruction?

The decision is ultimately ours. No one else can choose the words that come out of our mouths. That is solely our responsibility. We cannot cast blame or point a finger at anyone else for the things we say. This is why self-control is so important to a life of faith. Because the things that pop into our heads don't necessarily have any business popping out of our mouths.

Sometimes it's not so much a problem with our tongues as it is with our hearts. As Jesus tells us in Matthew 12:34, "the mouth speaks what the heart is full of." If the words flowing from your mouth are constantly negative or angry or hurtful, what does that say about the state of your heart?

Our children are so vulnerable, so the way we speak to them is extremely important. Their hearts are malleable and tender, and our words have the power to shape them forever. Will we kindle flames of love inside their hearts, or will we allow our words to burn their self-esteem to ashes?

Maybe someone else's words have hurt you deeply, leaving behind lingering wounds. If that's the case, then I'm so sorry for the pain you've experienced. I know how devastating that can be, especially if those words were spoken by someone you love. But I also want you to know that you can be healed from those wounds. Jesus will fill those holes in your heart – all you have to do is ask. He can make beauty from those ashes, sister. Don't let the wounds fester. Let Him make you whole again.

One other thing I would like to add to this is that we cannot allow our own pain to overflow to our children. We can't hurt them out of our own pain. We must choose to break toxic cycles and form healthy ones in their place. Our children's hearts are depending on it.

Hurting people hurt people, but healed people heal people. Use your pain to bring beauty to someone else's story. Let Jesus shine in the way you speak. Go light those fires of love!

Precious Jesus, please fill the holes in my heart left behind by careless words. Heal me from the pain I've felt from things people have said to me. Lord, help me not to continue the cycle of hurting people with my words. Let me speak life and joy and beauty into others' lives. I pray my words fill my children's hearts with love. Lord, thank you for your goodness and your grace. You are all I need.

In Jesus' Name, Amen

DAY 50

And let our people also learn to maintain good works, to meet urgent needs, that they may not be unfruitful.
Titus 3:14 NKJV

Maintaining good works seems to be a recurring theme in many of the verses we've touched on. While it's true that we are not saved by our works (Ephesians 2:8-9), it's also true that faith without works is dead (James 2:17). Good works are a necessary and important part of living a fruitful life.

Honestly, I don't see how we can exhibit the fruit of the Spirit without maintaining good works. They go hand in hand, kind of like peanut butter and jelly. They just make sense together. My kids can confirm this, because peanut butter and jelly sandwiches remain one of their favorite foods.

How can we display love or kindness or goodness or gentleness if we are not actively engaged in good works? That doesn't make sense. Good works are a natural outflow of the work of the Spirit in our hearts. If we are filled with Him, then He will naturally pour out of us.

I want to live a fruitful life that shows the love of Christ to others, and I want my family to be the greatest recipients of that love. I don't want them to get the worst of me or my leftovers after I've loved on everyone else. No, I want my family to get the best of me – the fullest and truest love that I can possibly give. And the only way I can offer that kind of love to them is by filling myself with the Spirit every single day.

Maintaining good works isn't something to be done only in public. It's not a show that we perform outside the walls of our houses, only to revert to selfishness as soon as we get home. Our homes should be equally filled with our good works. Our families should be smothered in our love and kindness. Otherwise, our good works to others are meaningless.

If our families are last on our list of kindness, we need to adjust our priorities. Spreading love to the world is important, yes, but our first and most important mission field is right inside our homes.

Holy Lord, help me to live a fruitful life. Let good works flow from my heart as I am filled with the Holy Spirit. God, I pray that my family would get the best of me. Help me to show them kindness and love and grace. Thank you for your strength and your joy. All that I am is because of you. You are everything to me. In Jesus' Name, Amen

Practice Patience

DAY 51

My brethren, count it all joy when you fall into various trials, knowing that the testing of your faith produces patience. But let patience have its perfect work, that you may be perfect and complete, lacking nothing.
James 1:2-4 NKJV

This life is full of various trials and storms. It is inevitable that we will face difficult seasons. But the Bible tells us to count it joy when our faith is tested because it's part of the pruning process.

Pruning isn't pleasant when you're in the midst of it, but the result is greater beauty and fuller life. Trials are never enjoyable when we're in the thick of them, but if we keep our eyes on Jesus through it all, it makes our faith stronger and our character more reflective of Him.

Tough seasons can do one of two things to the family unit – they can bring us closer together, or they can tear us all apart. It's not by chance that either of these things happens, but rather a result of how we react to our trials. Yes, it takes effort on the part of everyone to stay united. One person alone cannot keep a family headed in the right direction. But that does not lessen the mother's role in setting that tone for everyone else.

When hard times come, fix your eyes on Jesus. Keep Him at the front and center of your heart. Run the race with Him in mind, knowing that He won't leave you for a second. Draw near to Him through your trials and lean on Him for your strength.

Persevering through trials is a tool to refine our families. When we cling to Jesus together, our faith is sharpened and our bonds are strengthened. The way we react to hardship has the ability to bring our families closer to God.

If you are facing difficult things today, keep your eyes on Jesus. Remember that He is pruning you and refining you. Remember also that He never asks you to face anything alone. He's right there with you, whatever you face, and He will bring you through it.

Let patience have its perfect work, and let Jesus be the King of your heart.

Gracious Lord Jesus, I need your strength today. Help me through the difficult things I must face. Give me patience so that I may be perfect and complete, lacking nothing as I keep my eyes on you. Lord, I trust you. You are in control. Help my family to grow stronger and closer as we cling to you together.
In Jesus' Name, Amen

DAY 52

"Therefore do not worry about tomorrow, for tomorrow will worry about itself. Each day has enough trouble of its own."
Matthew 6:34 NIV

If you're anything like me, you probably have a million things on your mind at any given moment. Usually, I'm worrying about things that haven't even happened yet. My thoughts run wild until worst case scenarios somehow become given facts inside my mind. Anxiety over the future becomes overwhelming, filling me with dread and robbing me of joy in the present.

I don't know why I want to rush ahead to tomorrow's problems. Most of the things I worry about never even happen, yet I continue to get stuck in the cycle of fretting over what-ifs.

But that is not life-giving, and it's not God's desire for me. He wants me to remain present in today – right now, this hour, this moment. There's a reason the Lord's prayer asks for daily bread. Not monthly bread, not yearly bread, not even weekly bread. Daily bread. Because He knows that human hearts can't handle more than a day at a time, and He wants us to rely on Him and trust Him for today.

He doesn't want us to jump ahead to the future in our thoughts. He's given us the precious gift of the present moment, so why would we ruin it by worrying about tomorrow? Tomorrow might not come, but today is already here.

Sometimes patience means waiting for something we want to happen, but sometimes it means not fretting over things we think *might* happen. It means trusting God with the future and focusing on right now.

I am not God, and tomorrow is not mine to behold. However, I have so graciously been given today, and what a glorious gift today is! A gift I should cherish and enjoy, not throw away by obsessing over tomorrow.

Make it your goal today to be present in the moment. Don't let your mind run away with thoughts of the future. Banish what-ifs from consuming any of your time.

Live today like the glorious gift that it is, and let tomorrow worry about itself.

Heavenly Father, you are God and I am not. I release tomorrow to your care. Help me to be present in each moment. Lord, I want to enjoy the precious gift of today. Thank you for this beautiful life, and thank you for giving me daily bread. I trust you, Lord.
In Jesus' Name, Amen

DAY 53

Be joyful in hope, patient in affliction, faithful in prayer.
Romans 12:12 NIV

Nobody likes waiting. Whether it's waiting on an upcoming vacation, waiting on payday, or waiting on results from a medical test, it's one of the most tortuous aspects of human existence. We want instant gratification, and we really don't like being told to wait.

However, waiting is an inevitable part of life that we simply have to accept. We teach our kids to be patient from a very young age, but are we practicing what we preach? Are we bearing the fruit of patience in our own daily lives?

Our children are watching us, and how we wait says a lot about our hearts. Are we grouchy and irritable when we have to wait, or do we choose to maintain joy and peace? Are we focused on the answers we're waiting for, or are our eyes fixed on the Lord? What is the greatest desire of our hearts?

If we long for Jesus more than anything else, then waiting for other things won't faze us. We can have joyful hope in seasons of waiting because we find our fulfillment in Christ alone. We can be patient in affliction, trusting that God will carry us and bring us through, believing that He alone is our strength. And we can be faithful in prayer, bringing our concerns and our worries to Him, laying our hearts before Him and letting Him take control.

Patience isn't just the ability to wait, but the ability to wait well. How you compose yourself while you wait is indicative of the posture of your heart.

A great way to make waiting easier is to spend regular time in the Bible. Something about those timeless words makes everything else fade away. Another way to lessen the anxiety of waiting is praising God for His goodness. If you're focused on being thankful, then waiting doesn't feel so much like a burden. A heart overflowing with gratitude is too full to allow anxious thoughts to boil over.

If you're waiting for something – whether it's something exciting or something scary – fix your eyes on Jesus. Be joyful in hope, patient in affliction, and faithful in prayer.

Embrace today with a heart of gratitude and praise. Don't worry in the waiting. Use the waiting to trust in Jesus more.

Father God, help me to be patient in affliction. Fill me with hope and joy and peace. Lord, I don't want to let worry rule my heart. I want to trust you so deeply that I'm not fazed by having to wait. Your plans are good, Lord. I know that full well. Thank you for your marvelous works. My life is in your hands. I am in awe of your goodness. Help me to show my children what it truly means to be patient.
In Jesus' Name, Amen

DAY 54

You need to persevere so that when you have done the will of God, you will receive what he has promised.
Hebrews 10:36 NIV

We've talked about waiting, and it's definitely hard. There's nothing pleasant about being told to wait, especially when we want answers or outcome *right now*.

There are some things we just won't have the answers to in this lifetime. Things we don't understand and likely never will. Hard questions that weigh on our hearts and minds, making us cry out to God for answers over and over again.

When we don't get those answers, it's tempting to think that He's not listening or He doesn't care. We feel isolated and forgotten, like we've been left alone to our sorrow and pain. But that's never the truth. We are always, always, always held in His hands. Just because He seems to be silent, that doesn't mean He isn't listening. And just because His answer doesn't come how we expect it to, that doesn't mean He doesn't care.

Our children may ask us hard questions. They may seek answers that we simply can't provide. In those moments, we must turn them to God's Word and remind them that He is always listening, He always cares, and He is always in control.

Heartbreak will come. Seasons of hardship and doubt will come. Days full of agonizing questions with seemingly no answers will come. But we know without a shadow of a doubt that our God is good and our God reigns. He is on the throne, and He has already granted our victory. Nothing on earth can take away the promise He has sealed in our hearts.

We may have to wait for answers beyond the time that we live on this earth, but we can rest assured that we will receive the promise in due time. We will see our Savior face to face, and all the things that plagued us during our earthly lives will wither and fade away.

With that blessed hope in mind, we can patiently endure whatever we face in this life. This world is not our home, and this life is only a mist (James 4:14). Soon it will be gone and all our troubles will cease. But the Word of God will never fade away, and that is our true and lasting hope.

Wonderful Lord, thank you for hearing my prayers. I know that you are always listening and that you always care. Not a single tear goes outside of your notice. You are a gracious and loving Father. Lord, help me to patiently endure this life so that I may receive the promise in due time. Help me to run the race so that I might receive the prize. God, you are all I need, now and forever. Holy is your Name.

In Jesus' Name, Amen

DAY 55

Wait on the Lord; be of good courage, and He shall strengthen your heart; wait, I say, on the Lord!
Psalm 27:14 NKJV

Wait on the Lord. It sounds so simple, so easy, so straightforward. But when you're in the trenches of life, fighting the battle, wondering how you're going to make it through the day, it's easy to forget to wait on the Lord.

When things are hard, we want to fix it. We want quick answers and easy solutions to make the pain go away. We don't want struggle or uncertainty. How much less do we enjoy seeing our children face those things.

It's awful watching your child learn a tough lesson. You want to jump in and fix it for them. You want to make it quicker and lessen their pain. You want to ease their struggle.

That's a beautiful instinct God instilled into mothers, but we can't always be the one to fix things. We don't always have the answers or solutions our kids need, and sometimes they simply have to learn the lesson on their own. There are things we just can't rescue them from, no matter how badly we want to.

What we can do, though, is encourage them to wait on the Lord and let Him be their strength. We can remind them to lean on Jesus in times of struggle and difficulty. We can point them to His Word again and again, and we should most definitely be on our knees in prayer for them. Most of all, we can lead by example by waiting on the Lord in our own times of uncertainty and leaning on His strength in our weakness.

Maybe we can't solve our kids' problems or save them from hard lessons, but we *can* wait on the Lord. We can entrust our children to Him, knowing that He is completing a good work in them. We can be of good courage because we trust our Lord and Savior.

He is a good Father who loves His children, and that includes our precious babies. He's got them. He won't ever leave their side.

Precious Jesus, thank you for the lessons you've taught me, and thank you for the lessons you're teaching my children. Lord, I pray that you would help us to wait on you. Give us your strength to stand on when life feels uncertain. Help us to be of good courage. God, you are in control. You are a good Father, and I trust you to care for my babies.
In Jesus' Name, Amen

Not of This World

DAY 56

Do not conform to the pattern of this world, but be transformed by the renewing of your mind. Then you will be able to test and approve what God's will is—his good, pleasing and perfect will.
Romans 12:2 NIV

When I was younger, I would bend myself to fit in. I would emulate whoever I was around so they would like me or accept me. I had no solid sense of identity because it fluctuated with whatever people thought of me. What I was missing was the fact that my true identity is rooted in Jesus – the One who never changes and who loves me no matter what.

It doesn't matter if you're ten years old or a grown woman; it's hard not to worry about what people think. It's equally hard not to go with the flow in order to fit in. But God's will for us is to be set apart. We are not meant to conform to the ways of the world. His will for us is to be transformed, and that means renewing our minds.

What does it mean to renew your mind? It means to focus on things above and fix your eyes on Jesus. It means replacing destructive thoughts with life-giving thoughts. It means filling your mind with God's Word and meditating on His promises. Rather than constantly being entertained by things the world has to offer, we need to carve out time to spend with Him. We cannot expect our minds to be Christlike if we aren't filling them with Christ.

Sometimes it's lonely being different. Sometimes, when you choose to stand firm in the truth, it feels like you're up against the world. But our true fulfillment doesn't come from relationships with other people. Our identity isn't found in friendships or marriage or social media presence. It's found in Christ and Christ alone.

The world is full of temptation and sin, and it's not always obvious when something isn't pleasing to God. Sometimes the devil wraps temptation up in a shiny package with a big bow, making it look like something we want or need. Keeping our minds on Jesus helps us to discern between what's meant for us and what we should leave behind or say no to.

This world is not our home, so it's not surprising that we don't belong. We aren't the same as the world, and that's okay. God has set us apart for His special purposes.

He has given us everything we need to serve Him well. It's up to us to focus our hearts and minds on His presence.

Lord Jesus, help me to be transformed by the renewing of my mind. Give me strength to resist the temptation of conforming to the ways of this world. Thank you for your guidance and words of wisdom in the Bible. Your Word is a lamp unto my feet and a light unto my path. Whether people accept me or not, I know that I am your beloved daughter, and that is all I need. You are my heart's desire. Let me be full of you.

In Jesus' Name, Amen

DAY 57

Do not follow the crowd in doing wrong.
Exodus 23:2a NIV

There's a quote I heard a long time ago that says, "What's right isn't always popular, and what's popular isn't always right." Honestly, that's so very true, but it can also be hard to live out.

Especially in today's world of influencers and cancel culture, our children are faced with so much pressure. There are hundreds and thousands of voices shouting at them from every side, telling them what to do. It's scary how impressionable young people are nowadays, and it's compounded by the world of social media. I believe that no generation has faced more peer pressure or social influence than the kids growing up right now.

That's why we have to take our responsibility as their mothers very seriously. We have to teach them that what's popular isn't always right. Our kids must learn to base their moral compass on the Bible and not anything else. Even if they lose friends or followers or face getting "canceled," they must be confident enough in their convictions to be able to stand their ground. We have to raise a generation of bold and courageous Christians who are willing to fight for their faith.

It's a tough lesson to learn, but we want our kids to follow Jesus, not the crowd. We want them to worry more about what's right than what's popular, and they won't learn these things unless we're intentional about having deep conversations with them. Not only that, but we must lead by example. It's not enough to just talk the talk; we must also walk the walk.

Let your kids witness you standing for truth. Let them see you choosing Jesus over the crowd. It's easier for them to do it themselves if they see it modeled on a regular basis. Set that strong standard while they're young, so they already know what to do when they're older.

Stand firm and let Jesus be your identity. It's the best identity you could ever hope to have!

Holy Father, help me to stand for truth. Give me strength to go against the crowd and choose what's right. Lord, fill my heart with peace so that other people's opinions won't matter to me. My identity is found in you, and in you I am whole and complete. Help me to instill this truth into my children so they may be bold and confident in their faith. Thank you for your presence and strength in my life.
In Jesus' Name, Amen

DAY 58

Do not be overcome by evil, but overcome evil with good.
Romans 12:21 NIV

The world tries to tell us we're wrong when we stand for truth. It calls us all kinds of ugly names and tries to silence our voices. We are considered hateful simply for believing God's Word.

The world calls good what is evil, so being truly good is rare. Refusing to conform to the lies of culture makes us stand out, and that can be pretty scary.

Still, the only real way to overcome evil is by refusing to give in to it. We have to keep being good, even when the world tries to snuff out our light. Even when it means we face ridicule and hatred and threats. We can't stoop to those levels or return hatred with hatred.

We have been called to overcome evil with good. Our goodness is the greatest weapon we have against the enemy. Living a life of faith in step with the Spirit is something he simply cannot overcome. When we face persecution – even to the point of losing our lives for our faith – we press on in the knowledge that our souls will receive the promise of eternal life. That is the greatest victory over evil.

Our culture is getting more and more hostile toward Christians, so we need to prepare our children to face persecution. They have to understand that a life of faith does not guarantee safety from hatred and scorn. We will face opposition when we stand for our faith, but we will also be held responsible for our response. When we are found faithful, we will be blessed by the words of our Savior saying, "Well done" (Matthew 25:21).

Isn't that so much greater than cowering in fear and hiding our faith? Living out the promise might mean hardship and oppression in our earthly lives, but that will pale in comparison to the glorious riches of eternity in the presence of our King.

Teach your children that this world is not their home. Make sure they know that evil is real, but that we can overcome evil with good. Perhaps it might seem like evil is winning while we're still here on this earth, but God will have the ultimate victory. That's what we're looking forward to as we live our lives for Christ.

Gracious Savior, thank you for the promise of eternity with you. Lord, I know that victory is yours. Help me to live a life of faith, one that radiates your goodness to everyone around me. Even when I face evil, help me to overcome it with good. You alone are good and true, so strengthen me to shine your light. No matter what comes in this life, it pales in comparison to my future eternity. Hallelujah!

In Jesus' Name, Amen

DAY 59

He has shown you, O man, what is good; and what does the Lord require of you but to do justly, to love mercy, and to walk humbly with your God?
Micah 6:8 NKJV

God has shown us what He wants from us. It's up to us to choose His ways or the world's ways. The choices we make matter because our family is watching. We set the tone for our household by the way we live our lives.

Walking humbly with God is usually the exact opposite of what society wants us to do. This isn't anything new, though maybe it's more obvious in the world today. From the very beginning, Christians have faced opposition. But He has shown us what is good, and He has given us the Spirit to help us live according to His Word.

He hasn't left us here to struggle through life all alone. He's not a God who expects us to figure everything out. He walks with us, right beside us, every single moment of every single day. His expectations aren't some mystery we have to sleuth out like Nancy Drew. They're written plain as day.

He never changes. He is always steady and true. His commands are not just rules we have to abide by. They're designed to keep us in rightness with Him and make our lives so much fuller and richer. His commands are not burdensome (1 John 5:3), but they are intended to be completed by walking in step with Him.

Life may be complicated, but surrendering to the Lord is simple. Note that I didn't say *easy*, but simple. It's not a puzzle we have to solve. All it takes is giving our hearts to Him. From there, we are enabled to put on our spiritual armor and face every battle, and we can live for His glory in a world that embraces darkness.

Let's lead our families in what is good. Let's do justly, love mercy, and walk humbly with God. He has shown us the way. All we have to do is follow Him.

Heavenly Father, thank you for the roadmap you've given me in your Word. Help me to live a life of goodness. Lord, let me walk humbly with you, guiding my family in a life that glorifies you. Strengthen me to face the battle today, donning my spiritual armor so that I can extinguish the enemy's flaming arrows. You alone are good, and I am in awe of your mercy. Thank you for your love and joy and peace. I am yours.
In Jesus' Name, Amen

DAY 60

For you were once darkness, but now you are light in the Lord. Walk as children of light.
Ephesians 5:8 NKJV

What a beautiful reminder this verse is! We have been pulled out of darkness and into His glorious light. We have no part in the darkness, and the darkness cannot overcome us. We are children of light!

This world needs our light. Our neighbors need our light. Our families need our light. So let it shine! Be bold, be courageous, be sincere and genuine in your love for others. Be the hands and feet of Jesus to a world in desperate need of hope.

Darkness is all around us, but we have no reason to fear because we are children of light. Our souls are bought and paid for by the precious blood of Jesus Christ, and nothing can ever take that away from us. We have the greatest gift and the greatest hope, so we should live in a way that shines. We should make the world want what we have.

Walking as children of the light is easier when we walk together, lifting each other up, sharing each other's joys and burdens along the way. We should be a source of encouragement and joy and peace to our fellow sisters in Christ. We should be a safe place for our children when they face questions and doubts. Being a light means walking in step with the Spirit, allowing Him to guide our steps and light our paths.

The world might try to snuff our light, but we know who wins the war. The light shines in the darkness, and the darkness has not overcome it (John 1:5). We will not be overcome. We will share in Christ's victory, so let us live victoriously.

Celebrate this glorious truth today as you go forth into the world. You are no longer overcome by darkness, but you are a child of light. You are a daughter of the King. You are His beloved treasure and you have hope in His Name.

Forever and always, you are His. Nothing will ever change that.

Lord Jesus, thank you for saving me from the darkness! I know that I am a child of the light. I have freedom and hope and joy in Your Name. You are everything to me, and I am nothing without you. Help me to walk in a way that shines your light to others. Let my life be evidence of your love. Nothing else compares to you, Lord. Victory is yours, and through you I am victorious. What a beautiful promise!
In Jesus' Name, Amen

AFTERWORD

I'm so glad you've joined me on this journey. I pray that you've been encouraged through each page in this book, and I hope you continue to find God's strength and joy as you embrace motherhood with a heart of praise.

He is always faithful and always true. Let His Word light the way as you lead your family well. You are never alone, mama. You are always held in His hands.

If you've enjoyed this devotional, please consider leaving a review so other moms can find and enjoy it too!

ACKNOWLEDGMENTS

Thank you first and foremost to my Lord and Savior, Jesus Christ. Without you I am nothing. Thank you for guiding me through writing this book. I give it to you as an offering of love. You alone are worthy of all my praise. To you be the glory.

To my amazing husband, thank you for supporting me and believing in my books. You inspire me to aim higher and work harder, and I'm so thankful for that. And I also love doing life with you. God was so kind to bring us together.

To my beautiful children, I hope you know that being your mom is the greatest gift. You are the reason this book exists, so thank you. You've shaped me more than you'll ever know, and I absolutely adore being your mother.

Finally, thank you to my wonderful friends, Jessica and Abby, who helped me with this project. I couldn't have done it without you. Your encouragement through this journey was such a blessing. I am so thankful for you both.

ABOUT THE AUTHOR

Kaelin Scott is a ranch wife and homeschool mom. She writes Christian romance novels as well as a monthly column in an online Christian women's magazine. Her mission is to write books that point people to Christ. When she's not writing or teaching, you can find her reading, playing ping-pong with her hubby, or enjoying the great outdoors.

You can find her other books on Amazon and Kindle.

www.ingramcontent.com/pod-product-compliance
Lightning Source LLC
LaVergne TN
LVHW010920110826
845149LV00013B/2429

* 9 7 9 8 9 9 0 8 7 7 5 1 1 *